AMERICA
FASCISM
AND
GOD

AMERICA
FASCISM
AND
GOD

Sermons from a Heretical Preacher

DAVIDSON LOEHR

CHELSEA GREEN PUBLISHING COMPANY
WHITE RIVER JUNCTION, VERMONT

Editor: Safir Ahmed
Managing Editor: Marcy Brant
Copy Editor: Cannon Labrie
Proofreader: Kate Mueller
Designer: Peter Holm, Sterling Hill Productions
Design Assistant: Daria Hoak, Sterling Hill Productions

Printed in Canada
First printing, August 2005
10 9 8 7 6 5 4 3 2 1

Recycled Paper
Chelsea Green sees publishing as a tool for cultural change and ecological stewardship.
We strive to align our book manufacturing practices with our editorial mission, and to
reduce the impact of our business enterprise on the environment. We print our books
and catalogs on chlorine-free recycled paper, using soy-based inks, whenever possible.
Chelsea Green is a member of the Green Press Initiative (www.greenpressinitiative.org),
a nonprofit coalition of publishers, manufacturers, and authors working to protect the
world's endangered forests and conserve natural resources.
   America, Fascism, and God was printed on Legacy Trade Book Natural, a 100 percent
post–consumer waste recycled, old growth forest–free paper supplied by Webcom.

Library of Congress Cataloging-in-Publication Data
Loehr, Davidson, 1942-
   America, fascism, and God : sermons from a heretical preacher / Davidson Loehr.
      p. cm.
   ISBN 1-931498-93-8 (pbk.)
   1. Religion and politics—United States—Sermons. 2. Capitalism—Religious
aspects—Sermons. 3. Fascism—United States—Sermons. 4. Sermons, American—21st
century. 5. Unitarian Universalist Association—Sermons. I. Title.
   BL2525.L64 2005
   261.7'0973--dc22

                              2005015844

Chelsea Green Publishing Company
Post Office Box 428
White River Junction, VT 05001
(800) 639-4099

www.chelseagreen.com

CONTENTS

PRELUDE

This small book exists because of a sermon I delivered on November 7, 2004, five days after the presidential election. Titled "Living under Fascism," it drew together what I thought were pretty obvious patterns—the simultaneous rise to power of plutocracy, imperialism, and fundamentalism—into an even larger pattern: the establishment of an American style of fascism, with logical implications that should be seen as terrifying.

I am concerned for this nation and for its soul; both are in serious trouble. The nation has revived the dangerous and arrogant policy of preemptive invasions of sovereign nations that have resources or locations we desire for our own economic ends—a policy last made infamous by Hitler's invasion of Poland in 1939. Our politicians have rushed to endorse, in our name, imperialistic ambitions too greedy and bloody to be defended by noble ideals. The media are so unquestioning, they seem like co-conspirators. And the churches seem to lack the vision and the courage to serve us or our highest ideals. When our politicians, our media, and our official religions cannot be trusted with our high ideals and tender mercies, we are in deep trouble. And the way back to democracy, freedom, and honest religion, if still possible, will be very hard.

This book was written for reasons as personal as they are faithful and patriotic. I was born in 1942 and grew up in a middle-class family in an America that was defined, I believed, by democracy, exalting the middle class, and upholding the highest moral and ethical values at home and abroad. I believed in that picture, and loved it.

Within a week after President John F. Kennedy's assassination, my local draft board increased its quota tenfold to prepare for the Vietnam buildup that Kennedy was planning to cancel when he was murdered. I was out of college for the semester repaying a school loan and was going to be drafted. So I enlisted and took it seriously. I graduated from the Army's best NCO academy in Bad Tolz, Germany, and from the Artillery Officer Candidate School. I served as an assistant brigade adjutant for a 4,000-man training brigade and was then sent to Vietnam. During what amounted to a job interview after arriving, my orders were changed, and I became the Vietnam Entertainment Officer, charged with meeting entertainers at the airport and taking them out to dinner on an expense account funded by profits from enlisted men's—but not officers'—clubs in Vietnam. More officially, our office arranged the itineraries of visiting shows and entertainers. Sharing an afternoon and a beer with Roy Rogers and Dale Evans was one of the thrills of my young life—though the little boy in me could hardly believe they really drank beer!

When a classmate from officer candidate school was decorated as a genuine war hero, I felt guilty and cowardly for not being in combat. I knew that if I returned home without having had the experience of war, I would not want to live with myself.

So I transferred to the field and spent my final seven months in Vietnam as combat photographer and press officer for the 17th Public Information Office, attached to the 11th Armored Cavalry Regiment in Xuan Loc. I was shot at, mortared, and have as a souvenir the live bullet that was aimed at my head when the North Vietnamese army officer squatting fifteen feet in front of me was killed by the two men beside me. I was not wounded, sometimes scared, and never heroic, though I did my job for my country and tried to do it well. As a result, my time in Vietnam—especially the last seven months—is sacred time for me. I wouldn't trade it for anything.

I believed in my country and learned that courage mostly consists in showing up for a war, rather than trying to avoid it through special entitlements or the bribes of privilege.

After returning in 1967, it took almost twenty years before I would acknowledge that we had absolutely no business in Vietnam, that the lives of our soldiers were lost for no decent purpose, and that the million or more Vietnamese we killed were the victims not of a just war, but of ignorant and arrogant slaughter.

After the war, I was far more lost than I knew. I stumbled through college, acquiring a degree in music, owned a photography studio, and then took up carpentry and drinking. In 1978, I felt the first real "calling" of my life: to the ministry. Not to "serve God," as it's romantically and misleadingly put, but to serve the ideals that symbols like America, democracy, and God rely on for their dignity and nobility. Honest religion addresses the most important questions in life—perhaps I wanted the experience of being in those "front lines."

I also wanted a good education. So rather than going to seminary, I got academic M.A. and Ph.D. degrees from the University of Chicago Divinity School. There, I found high ideals served with dedication and courage—which is pretty close to what is, for me, the sacred center of life. I knew I was an alcoholic, and that I wasn't likely to get through a tough graduate school half-soused. A month before classes began, I quit drinking and smoking on my own, bolstered by the strength of this new calling.

I have always thought of orthodoxies of all kinds as the lowest common denominator of people who have not found a religion but joined a potentially dangerous club. That makes me a natural-born heretic. People think heresy is a bad thing, but it's not. It comes from a Greek word meaning "to choose." Why is it seen as wrong to choose? Because some arrogant little groups declared that the choices were closed, because they had this "God" business all figured out. Those who aren't through choosing are then, by definition, heretics.

I chose religion as a profession because it seemed to be the only discipline specifically concerned with articulating and serving life's most enduring ideals, dynamics, and allegiances—symbolized as gods. I chose the ministry because, while I dearly loved the intellectual discussions at Chicago, academia often and easily becomes lost in thoughts about thoughts about thoughts. I wanted the thoughts dragged down to earth, where they had to survive testing by real people struggling in real lives.

Yet my interest in abstractions remains strong and is the main reason I'm not involved in—and don't like—politics. Politics is, by definition and necessity, the unending struggle for one partial vision to gain power over other partial visions. But the allegiance to partial visions is what I see as our problem, not our solution. Yes, religions have probably done as much harm as good—especially when they are given an army. Religions are routinely hijacked by dogmatic preachers and demagogic politicians who want to enslave people rather than empower them. Still, I think religion is the best place to start.

But I'm a heretic, through and through. If I were a Presbyterian, I would rail against Presbyterianism and argue that we're not meant to be Presbyterians, or even Christians; we're just meant to love one another and to work for justice—which can be defined as love at a distance. I considered entering the ministry in the

United Church of Christ, probably America's most liberal Protestant denomination. But I have never been a Christian. I have been a fellow in the Jesus Seminar since 1991 because I like many of the teachings of the man Jesus. I like the religion *of* Jesus. But I have never liked the religion *about* Jesus, created by Peter, Paul, and the early Church Fathers.

So, while I ply my ministerial trade under the umbrella of the Unitarian Universalist Association, I describe myself as a religious liberal, but *not* a Unitarian Universalist. I see this tiny movement as a microcosm of what's wrong with the social and political left in America. Its center is political rather than religious, and it seems to swallow whole every liberal fad that comes down the road. Still, it offers more freedom than any other religious association, and there is probably no other home as suitable for a heretic like me.

For the past twenty years, I have tried to help the people I'm privileged to serve become better people, partners, parents, and public citizens. We must try to create noble humans from the raw material we're born with—material that can become good, evil, deep, shallow, a blessing, or a curse, depending on how seriously we take the challenge of reaching our fullest human potential and being a healthy presence in the world as we pass through it. Our job is to make a positive difference for ourselves, our family and friends, and our larger community.

If that doesn't sound religious, it should; it's just expressed in ordinary language, rather than cloaked in religious jargon. It can easily be translated into the club talk of any of the world's religions. It is trying to realize our Buddha-nature, trying to grow the God-seed within us, as the Christian Meister Eckhart put it. It is trying to find, and become part of, the Tao—the Way. It is taking seriously the Hindu teaching that our atman, or soul, is most essentially part of Brahman, the creative and sustaining forces of the universe. Each bit of club talk is an idiom of expression peculiar to its home religion and communicates most readily—sometimes *only*—with those who are "in the club." Ordinary language, on the other hand, pulls back the curtain to see if we actually have any idea what we're talking about, in ways that can communicate with the vast majority of humans in all times and places. Ordinary language is the language of the most honest religion, and it's what I'll try to use throughout this book of sermons.

Yes, sermons. But you might ask: Aren't sermons just trying to trick you into buying something you shouldn't buy? They preach from a "confessional truth," which means one so small it can fit within the biases of this or that religion—right?

The answer to these questions is yes, if the sermons are expressed in jargon. But if they are done in plain talk and open to all questions and criticisms, then the answer is that sermons, honestly done, are trying to reconnect us with those deep and profound values that can help us grow more whole and authentic. In the same way, prayers are often little more than tacky requests for personal favors we haven't earned, from a God we presume is too stupid to see through us. But done honestly, a prayer is a semipoetic effort to create an atmosphere of honesty and humility, as we stand aware of our failings and weaknesses, acknowledging our flaws and asking—asking ourselves—that we might become better people than we have been.

Religion isn't about God; it's about growing more whole and more authentic. I'm a religious liberal because it is the most honest and courageous of all religious styles—and has been for around 2,500 years.

This book isn't so much a warning as it is an autopsy. The America that most of us loved has been cleverly and systematically murdered to feed the monetary and imperialistic hunger of some of our greediest people. The results of this death are easy to measure. The United States is 49th in the world in literacy and 28th out of 40 countries in mathematical literacy. Europe surpassed the United States in the mid-1990s as the largest producer of scientific literature. The World Health Organization has ranked us 37th in the quality of health care and 54th in the fairness of health care; the United States and South Africa are the only two developed countries that do not provide health care for all their citizens. About 18,000 Americans die each year because they have no health insurance (that's six times the number of people killed on 9/11). U.S. childhood poverty now ranks 22nd among 23 developed nations (Mexico ranks last). American women are 70 percent more likely to die in childbirth than European women. About 3.6 million Americans ran out of unemployment insurance in 2004; 1.8 million (one in five) unemployed workers are jobless for more than six months. One-third of all U.S. children are born out of wedlock, and one-half of all U.S. children will live in a one-parent household. Meanwhile, Americans now spend more money on gambling than on movies, videos, DVDs, music, and books combined. Nearly one out of four Americans believes that using violence to get what they want is acceptable. A related fact is that nearly 900,000 children were abused or neglected in 2002. (The above statistics came from various online sources, including the *New York Times* and an article by Michael Ventura called "No. 1?" in the *Austin Chronicle*, January 31, 2005.)

These and other statistics paint a picture of a nation whose money, heart, and soul have been hijacked by a coalition of those willing to enslave rather than empower us. The wholesale return to command-and-control governments is happening not only in America, but also in organized religions—with the rise of fundamentalism and the election of the former Hitler Youth member

Cardinal Ratzinger as the new pope, and with our continued insistence on invading any country with oil or location we desire, killing hundreds of thousands of people along the way as though they were somehow less precious than we are.

It's easy to lose hope. I remember the great American philosopher Lily Tomlin saying "No matter how cynical I get, I just can't keep up!" But the antidote to cynicism is the combination of hope, vision, and courage, and that's the only path worth considering.

We need honesty and courage now more than at any time in my life, because the fragile experiment in American democracy has been ended by three powerful forces—the manipulative perversions of money, power, and religion. Our economy is now defined by a rapacious form of plutocracy that robs the earners to give to the owners. Our government and our armies are driven by murderous dreams of worldwide domination. And the most profound enemy of honest religion and honest government is the literalistic form of religion known as fundamentalism.

Fundamentalism is always a natural ally of greed, brutality, and war, as it has now become in America. When you hear men like Pat Robertson and Jerry Falwell say that rich people shouldn't be taxed, that there should be no welfare programs for the poor, and that we should hunt down terrorists and "blow them away in the name of the Lord," you are as far from honest religion—and as far from simple human decency—as you can get. For the record, it is also not what Jesus would do.

All three of these powerful streams—plutocracy, imperialism, and fundamentalism—have brought us closer to protofascism, moving toward the full-blown thing.

By attacking the leaders in American politics, religion, and the media, I do not mean to attack the vast majority of Americans who have been misled by them. In all political and religious groups—and in the unmentioned majority of Americans who do not go to church regularly at all—we find equally intelligent, caring, and moral people. And we need them all, because on the whole, people are good. We come into the world with both original sins and gifts to offer. Our chief sin is taking ourselves and our views too seriously and worshiping them. Our chief gift is a good heart, a good commonsense mind, and immense reserves of dedication and courage, once we have been awakened.

If this sounds like preaching, it's because I'm a preacher. I want to convert you so we can move toward the more honest and empowering picture of America that has been stolen from us—brilliantly, brutally, almost completely—during the past few decades.

For all three streams that flow into the river of "America"—imperialism, plutocracy, and fundamentalism—have become too polluted to sustain life. We need to gain the insight and the courage to make different choices—heretical choices—that might once again lead us to see, love, yearn for, demand, and work toward what Abraham Lincoln called "the better angels of our nature," rather than the low, mean, thieving, and murderous ones that now define this country we love.

Today, the Democratic Party seems no more helpful than the other one. They both function like preowned vehicles to chauffeur around the special interests of large corporations and the greedy rich. So maybe the spirit of liberal politics will need to don a new costume—progressivism, perhaps. These are political debates that will be enriched by the inclusion of many voices.

But they are not *just* political debates. More fundamentally and profoundly, they are *religious* debates over the deep values and allegiances that really guide our country and our laws. Bad actions are the fruits of bad trees, and it is not so much our politics, but our religion that we need to reclaim. When gods die, their corpses aren't buried right away. They linger on for centuries, as the hand puppets of the worst kind of charlatans and demagogues who know that by controlling a society's most emotionally laden symbols they can control much of society itself.

This isn't a new insight. During the reign of the Roman Empire, Seneca wrote, "Religion is regarded by the common people as true, by the wise as false, and by the rulers as useful." Old Seneca would see little today that would surprise him.

The great German poet Goethe once said that those who know only one language don't really know *any* language. That's because when we only know one way to express things, we come to think that's the way things really are. That's why I believe only ordinary language—plain talk—can show us the differences and similarities among the many political and religious ideologies in our profoundly pluralistic world.

By appealing to those who are more comfortable discussing their ultimate values in ordinary language, I am not appealing to the fringes, but to the vast majority of Americans. For over sixty years, sociological studies have been assuring us that about 40 percent of Americans attend church regularly—which means 60 percent of Americans *don't*. A study published in the *Christian Century* in 1998 showed the serious overreporting on issues like these and suggested the far more likely figure that 20 percent of Americans actually attend church regularly. Kirk Hadaway, who has written a dozen books on congregational structures and dynamics, told me that he estimates the average church attendance for all faiths in America to be 21 to 22 percent of the total population. That means four of every five Americans do *not* attend church regularly. They have become our new "silent majority."

This book is written for them. But it is also written for all "believers" and those in the religious professions who wish there were ways to convert their institutions to the high, noble, and challenging visions of people like Lao-Tzu, Confucius, the Hebrew prophets, Buddha, Jesus, Muhammad, Rumi, Krishnamurti, and the other greatest philosophers, sages, and poets of history. I think that's a majority of those who consider themselves religious and those who consider themselves moral and ethical, though not religious.

Henry Kissinger once said the trouble with politicians is that 90 percent of them give the other 10 percent a bad name. Now much the same can be said of religious professionals. Even if they have not betrayed their religion by reducing their God to the level of their own bigotries or calling for the murder of people in God's name—even if they haven't actively betrayed their high callings, the vast majority of ministers have passively betrayed them, by sitting silently by, offering syrupy words rather than challenging ones. That is why the way back toward our fuller humanity now requires that decent people reframe and reclaim our highest ideals from both politicians and clergy.

This sounds radical, even revolutionary. It both is, and is not.

It is revolutionary, in the sense that restoring America to a democracy—if it can even be done—and holding professional clergy accountable to higher values than they are serving can only be done if ordinary people reclaim these in plain talk. If it were actually to happen, it would feel revolutionary.

On the other hand, the act of holding preachers and politicians to a higher standard than they want to serve—this has marked the entire history of both religion and politics. It is the conflict between the religion of the priests (ancient and modern) and the religion of the prophets. It is the vast difference between the religion *of* Jesus and the religion *about* him: the religion of the baby and the cross.

In the Hebrew Bible, this was the role taken by the prophets. Amos, Jeremiah, Hosea, Micah, and the others were all opposing the priests of their day, in the name of higher values. And they didn't express the values in precious religious language, but in ordinary language. Amos said God would punish his people "because they sell the righteous for silver, and the needy for a pair of shoes . . ." (Amos 2:6, RSV). He also declared that God would punish his people "because they have ripped up women with child in Gilead, that they might enlarge their border" (Amos 1:13). That's not theological jargon; it's plain talk that everyone can understand easily. Unless our preachers, politicians, and media apply these words to our illegal and murderous invasion of Iraq and the vicious economy inflicted on the world by our corporations, the WTO, and NAFTA, they are not serving any ideals worth serving, and the people must reclaim these ideals to keep them from withering and dying.

When a colleague suggested that my sermon "Living under Fascism," which was listed on several hundred websites, was the most widely read liberal sermon of the past thirty or forty years, he meant it as a compliment. I heard it as a sad indictment of religion in our times, because it says that no one would even *think* of sermons as vehicles of relevance or truth.

When I delivered that sermon, several of our church's members stayed away, as they stayed away from most sermons in which I talked about politics, the economy, and the war. Most ministers know the witty quip that a preacher's job is "to comfort the afflicted, and afflict the comfortable." Still, I don't blame people for hoping their church will be a source of comfort rather than affliction. Life's challenging enough without wondering if you'll leave church feeling worse than when you came in.

But we must engage the spirit of our times and the gods being served by our society, or else religion is too cowardly to respect. The leaders of the church I serve supported my confrontational style and absorbed the loss of thousands of dollars in pledges.

Every minister knows how rare it is to have such church leaders—especially when they actually represent the church's culture! So I begin by expressing my deep personal admiration and gratitude to the leaders and members of the First Unitarian Universalist Church of Austin, Texas. It is a privilege to serve you—all of you.

A "free pulpit" isn't free, and honest religion is always heretical. Heresy isn't a bad word. Sometimes it is the only place left where you can find the quality of spirit that was once rightfully called Holy.

See if I can persuade you.

PART ONE

GOD

I

The ABC of Religion
SEPTEMBER 10, 2000

Story: "The ABC of Music"

A. A girl walked down a sidewalk as she had many times before, when she suddenly noticed a new building. Looking in the window, she saw an odd sight. There was a girl, about her age, standing in a far room of the building, doing what looked like a kind of dance, or at least a dance done from the waist up, for her feet hardly moved at all. She was holding a rod in her hands, out to her right side, and she seemed to have the other end of the rod in her mouth, biting it, or at least chewing on it. As she bit it, she moved a little, a kind of gentle swaying motion. The girl outside could not see clearly, for the window was dirty, or cloudy. Still, it was the strangest sight! She began stopping by this building each day to watch the dance, always about the same, and soon found herself wondering whether she wasn't looking into the window of some kind of a hospital—a hospital where they put people who did these slow dances while biting metal rods.

B. One day when she walked by, the window was open. And now, when the girl looked in, she could see clearly, and she could hear. And she heard the sound of a flute. It was a flute player, not a dancer, and the point of it all had not been the movement, but the music, which the

3

girl had never heard before. "Aha," said the girl, "now I understand!" Then, no longer interested by the spectacle, she turned to leave.

C. But the flute player saw her and called out to her. Surprised, the girl stayed by the window as the other girl approached. "Here," said the flute player when she reached the open window, "wouldn't you like to play? This is yours, after all, and it is your turn now." With that, she handed the flute through the open window to the girl who had, until then, been only a spectator. And then the flute player disappeared, the whole building disappeared, and the little girl found herself standing there with her whole life still ahead of her, holding a flute—and trying to remember the movements, and the music.

Reading Religious Scriptures

Since fundamentalists have now taught many Americans what "religion" is, most of these people think that sacred scriptures were written to be read literally. But the best religious thinkers—in every religion of which I'm aware—have always been clear that literalism is the mortal enemy of all honest religion. For now, I'll just introduce you to some of the writings of an early third-century Christian writer known as Origen. He was a powerful thinker: some of his books are still in print and taught in graduate religion programs. His influence on Western religion has been significant. Saint Jerome called him "The greatest teacher of the Church after the apostles." He was born about A.D. 185, probably in Alexandria. He died, after imprisonment and extended torture, in 254. The following remarks are adapted from his book called *On First Principles*.

He says that in the Bible, divine things are communicated to people somewhat obscurely and are the more hidden in proportion to the unbelief or unworthiness of the inquirer. He writes that some of "the more simple believers" believe such things about God that not even the most unjust and savage of men would believe. And the reason why they can't understand Scripture in any profound way is that they don't understand Scripture in its *spiritual* sense, but only in its literal sense.

There are three layers of meaning in Scripture, he says, each suited to different degrees of intellectual development and spiritual maturity:

A. "The simplest folk" may get something out of the *body* of the Scriptures (which is what Origen calls the common and literal interpretation).

B. Those who have begun to make a little progress and are able to see a bit more than that may be fed by the *soul* of the Scriptures. This means the symbolic or metaphorical understanding of things: to seek insights into life, into who we are and how we should live. I would define "liberal religion" in all traditions as this level of understanding.

C. Those who are most advanced in both mind and spirit may finally understand the *spiritual* dimension of Scripture: those parts that are said to have been written, poetically speaking, under the inspiration of the Holy Spirit. These are the believers who are led to live sacred lives, rather than merely understand sacred words.

How then should we understand sacred scriptures? We should understand them by knowing that these mysteries were portrayed *figuratively* through stories of what *seemed* to be human deeds and the handing down of laws and commandments. But the real messages are hidden and take some work to uncover. This protects them from what we might call casual tourists and trinket-hunters. (Origen wrote of people who would trample upon these mysteries.) But according to Origen, the real insights of Scripture were only for those willing to do the hard personal work to gain them. The deep truths of religion—all of which were for living more wisely and well here and now—were not pearls to be cast before swine, as Jesus put it. If we believe Scriptures to be inspired by God, then we must seek a meaning *worthy* of God, a meaning always concealed under the language of an ordinary narrative that points in a different direction, as Origen put it.

This is the key: we should try to discover in the Scriptures that we believe to be *inspired* by God a meaning that is *worthy* of God. And here Origen believes the Holy Spirit can guide us, for it urges us, by the impossibility of the literal sense, to an examination of the *inner* meanings of Scripture.

In summary, all our reading of sacred scriptures must be guided by two considerations. We are seeking, with honest minds and pure hearts, for those things that are both *useful to us* and *worthy of God*. If we keep these things in mind, we shall not easily be misled.

Sermon: The ABC of Religion

It's surprising how many times the study of religion seems to have three levels, three stages of understanding—like the little story of the flute player:

A. The literal or "factual" level; like standing outside a closed window thinking that the meaning of the sight must be in the motions because that's all you can see.

B. The metaphorical or intellectual level; like opening the window and discovering the motions were secondary to the music, which was the real point of it all.

C. The existential or personal level; when someone hands you the flute, and you realize that you are not just a "spectator" in life, that it is your turn to play.

When I began studying religion in graduate school, I had no previous religious education—no undergraduate courses and very little knowledge of the Bible or other religious texts. I didn't have much of a notion of what religion was about, beyond the general understanding that, on the surface, religion seems to be concerned with gods or goddesses and that, on a deeper level, it's concerned with important questions about life. Beyond that, I wasn't sure what to expect.

What I didn't expect was to read the writings of thinkers like Origen, which we were exposed to almost immediately. I knew that modern liberals looked on the Bible and other sacred scriptures as symbols, metaphors, and myths that depicted life in poetic imagery and stories, but I never knew that the better religious thinkers had been saying this for over 2,000 years. So the first time I read the writings of people like Origen, I could hardly believe it. I wondered why people weren't told this in church, if religion is supposed to be about truth that can set you free.

Here was a voice from almost 1,800 years ago saying that reading religious scriptures literally is the unimaginative or uneducated sort of thing that children do. If you're serious about understanding this subject, he was saying, the literal level isn't even worth bothering with, because it misses the whole point of religion. The real concerns of religion can only be understood if you grow beyond that literal level and realize that all scriptures are speaking in poetic images about a different level entirely—"concealed under the language of an ordinary narrative that points in a different direction," as Origen put it.

It was almost as though the real meanings had been protected from casual observers by being written in the code—the same code found in most great literature and poetry—of symbols and metaphors, allegories and myths. We learned, over and over and over again in graduate school, that a literal reading of any religious scripture, like a literal reading of good poetry or fiction, is unacceptable: it is useless and unworthy of the subject of religion. It is like watching a flute player through a closed and cloudy window. This was the first level, the A level, of approaching any great literature, including religious literature.

The second level, the B level, which Origen had called the "soul" of sacred scriptures, showed us that the great religious writings are really concerned with existential insights into the nature of life itself. The same is true of music, poetry, and all the rest of the arts.

But all of a sudden, when you move from level A to level B and then look at the history and writings of religion again, *everything* changes. Because if religious writings are only taken on a literal level, then they are easy to dismiss, and we can feel smart and smug, imagining that all those old writers were just shallow fools compared to us! But here they are, nearly 2,000 years ago, describing the literal approach to religious scriptures as childish and unfit for adults, especially for serious students of religion.

Nor was this man Origen alone. He was not the exception, but the *rule*. Nearly *all* the great thinkers were that dismissive of literal readings of Scripture. Take, for instance, Saint Augustine, a powerful and influential writer in the fifth century who nearly defined Roman Catholicism for a thousand years. He was considered the grandfather of the Protestant Reformation, because

Martin Luther was an Augustinian monk, strongly influenced by his works, and nearly a third of John Calvin's major theological work was adapted from Augustine's writings. You might think Augustine was busy cranking out creeds, but it is not what you find when you read him. Instead, you find things like this:

> Some people . . . imagine God as a kind of man or as a vast bodily substance endowed with power, who by some new and sudden decision created heaven and earth. . . . When these people hear that God said "Let such and such be made," and accordingly it was made, they think . . . that once the words had been pronounced, whatever was ordered to come into existence immediately did so. Any other thoughts which occur to them are limited in the same way by their attachment to the familiar material world around them. These people are still like children. But the very simplicity of the language of Scripture sustains them in their weakness as a mother cradles an infant in her lap. But there are others for whom the words of Scripture are no longer a nest but a leafy orchard, where they see the hidden fruit. They fly about it in joy, breaking into song as they gaze at the fruit and feed upon it. (*Confessions*, trans. R. S. Pine-Coffin, Penguin Classics, 304.)

If you are a student of the arts, if you love the humanities, this kind of writing and this kind of insight has an immediate appeal to you. It is like the window has opened, and you hear the music. The "instruments" here are religious scriptures, in all traditions, and one of the most important things you learn in a good religious education is that the symbols, stories, legends, and myths of religion are meant to make music, not dogma. They are about life, not belief. And if you just stay on the surface, you miss all of that: you miss the "spirit" that inspired those scriptures.

Annie Dillard tells a story in which she describes how she learned to split wood. At first, she says that she aimed at the tops of the logs, but all she produced were useless slivers of wood. Later she learned to aim for the block—past the target—to get the job done. Understanding religion is like that. While there are some things that have merely literal meanings lying just on the surface, there aren't many and they aren't very important. You have to aim beyond the words, to the more fundamental truths lying beneath them.

You may wonder why writers don't just say what they mean—not only in religious literature but in all literature. Take a book like John Steinbeck's *The Grapes of Wrath*, for instance. Many people have taught that Steinbeck was saying that the American Dream was only for the rich few, carried on the backs of the poor, and that the only nourishment most of us will find is what little milk of human kindness we can give to one another. Well then, why didn't he just say so, instead of writing a whole book?

Or take F. Scott Fitzgerald's novel *The Great Gatsby*, the book some have called the greatest American novel: Why didn't he simply say that the American Dream isn't enough to sustain a life, even for the rich? Why did he have to invent all those characters, and all those happenings?

These are all questions from level A. And the answer, which can only come from level B, is that the truth of literature, including religious literature, is not a truth about the characters in the stories but about life. And truths about life are most clear and most useful when told in stories that recreate a living context for them: stories that we can identify with, stories we can feel.

And so once you get it, you think "Aha, now I understand!" like the girl watching the flute player. And you go out to teach or preach religion as great literature, and you think you've got it now.

But then you think of what Origen wrote in his third level, about "the believers who are led to live sacred lives, rather than merely understanding sacred words." This third level, level C, means that religion is, at bottom, not an intellectual issue at all, but an *existential* one: it is our *lives* that are at stake here. If we live only once, if all the heavens and hells in all the world's religions are metaphors for qualities of life here and now, and if this really is all there is, then we're not talking about mind games. We're talking about the fact that life is short, it matters a lot how we live it, and there aren't many clear guidebooks.

I remember how Saint Paul's statement that "we work out our salvation in fear and trembling" took on entirely different meanings in a seminar where we were asked how we were working out our salvation. There was not a person in the classroom who believed in a literal or supernatural religion. We all knew that both life and religion are about the here and now. But then whatever salvation there is to be is also here and now. How are we to work it out?

We were mostly concerned with education, whether we were going into college teaching or into the ministry. But the questions about what makes life worth living are powerful questions in any area.

There was a nineteenth-century Danish existentialist named Søren Kierkegaard who once wrote about the kinds of games we play with religious beliefs when we keep them as merely intellectual pursuits unrelated to our real lives. We are like passengers on a ship, he said, who spend their time arranging the deck chairs in neat little rows. And this, said Kierkegaard, is supremely funny: not because neat little rows are bad, but because the ship is sinking.

Every day, all the time, the ship is sinking. We move through our lives toward that moment when we shall not move at all. Life isn't a snapshot; it's a motion picture, moving toward its ending. We stand there with the flute in our hands, our life before us, not sure just what the movements were supposed to be, or how the music is supposed to sound.

Until there is that sense of anxiety, until there is that sense of "fear and trembling," the flute hasn't been placed in our hands, and we haven't really felt the full impact of what this religion business is about.

This is the third level of religion, level C, the level where it finally dawns on us that every religious scripture has been written from the yearnings of the human soul, yearnings we all have.

We have a funny way of thinking about religion, especially among educated folks. We usually think of a religion as a collection of pseudo-intellectual propositions. We judge the acceptability of those propositions, then accept or reject the parts of the religion that fit our understanding of what is intellectually coherent and defensible.

In other words—and this is quite ironic—religious liberals often tend to operate at about the same level as Christian fundamentalists. By thinking that religion is about belief, we tend to take it at the same literal level that fundamentalists do, though we oppose them. They say God is some sort of a critter somewhere up there, heaven is a literal place we go after we die, and so on. Often, we also take our religion at the same level. Yes, we say, the terms of traditional religion are talking about a God who is some sort of a critter somewhere up there, and yes, heaven is referring to a literal place we're supposed to go after we die. In other words, it is all literal and it is all false.

Like the fundamentalists, most of those who attack them operate at the same level, level A. And we must grant these honest critiques their due. There is no "eternal life" involving time or space. No deity is going to give us a chance to do it right after we're dead. These are superstitions that have been used to control and mislead believers forever. Religion isn't about God or gods, though it is often written to *sound* that way. Religion is about how to live more wisely and well here and now. It has no end runs around science to offer. Its great myths and insights are about living more authentic lives. Religions that can't rise to this level of honesty with us cannot be trusted with our minds or our souls.

If you think about it, concepts like atheism and agnosticism and questions about whether or not you "believe in" God are only coherent at the literalist, fundamentalist level. Once you understand that the key terms of religion are symbolic, allegorical, and metaphorical, then words like "atheism" simply become incoherent, don't they? After all: if God is love, then what does it mean to be an atheist? Or an agnostic?

Perhaps religion is really as easy, and as hard, as ABC:

A. Have we grown past the literal level? That is the question posed to us at level A. Have we understood that all the talk of gods and angels, heavens and hells, deaths and resurrections, and the rest of it, doesn't really have anything to do with actual gods, angels, heavens, hells, deaths, or resurrections? If not, then we fail before we even begin. We fail to understand what religion is about. We stand outside the closed window, watching the odd movements inside, and not hearing the music.

B. At level B, we are asked a second question: Can we now begin to hear religion in a new way? Can we listen to its teachings as messages about life expressed in the poetic code language of symbols, myths, allegories, and metaphors? If so, we can gain entrance to this second

God

level of religion. Once the window is opened and we can hear the music, then we need to reframe our earlier understanding of those strange movements we had been watching from the outside. If the point of it all isn't "going through the motions" but "making music," then what is religion about? How now do we understand it?

C. And at level C, it all changes again. For just when we begin to think that we've mastered this religion business, the flute is handed to us through that open window. Now we are faced with our own life and new questions. What are the gods we've served with our lives, and what kind of a life have they led us to? Is it useful to us? Is it worthy of God? There is so much on the line, and so little to stand on that is absolutely certain. It no longer even needs to involve *religion* any more. It is about life, integrity, authenticity, and courage. And we can address all those "ultimate concerns" in ordinary language—in ways that everyone can understand.

So here we are. We stand with that flute in our hands. Ahead of us lies the rest of our life. We finally understand that it is our turn to make the music.

This book is about more than the ABCs of religion. It is about the ABCs of reframing and reclaiming our highest and noblest ideals and values. It is about reclaiming them from our politicians, bureaucrats, and media and from ministers and churches who don't, won't, or can't serve these ideals and values with candor and courage.

In his book *Don't Think of an Elephant*, George Lakoff says that "progressives" need to reclaim and reframe the direction of their country by grounding their politics in "values." I want to add to that by saying the values we need for our lives and our country are not political, but moral and ethical. They are the values our religions were supposed to serve. But in twenty-first-century America, very few of our churches or ministers actually serve our highest ideals any longer. The symbols of all three Western religions—Judaism, Christianity, and Islam—have been hijacked by some of our worst preachers and theologians and turned into sanctions for hateful bigotries and military slaughters of all kinds.

In revulsion and reaction, many have chosen to think of themselves as "secular." In some ways, it is a good choice. But they—especially religious and political liberals—have usually thrown out the baby with the bathwater. It is fine to reject religious language. But it is disastrous to throw out the concern for articulating the highest values of which we are capable. I want to persuade you to reclaim that search for those highest ideals and values—and to put them in plain talk, so we actually know what we're talking about.

Note: I used several translations from the Latin and Greek of Origen's *On First Principles,* book IV, chapter 2, including the translation by Rowan A. Greer in *Origen,* in the *Classics of Western Spirituality* series published by Paulist Press, 1979.

2

God as a Hand Puppet

FEBRUARY 16, 2003

How often have you even thought of reconsidering the concept of God?

God is discussed in our culture like a cartoon character, like a critter. Almost the only "theological" question anyone thinks to ask is "Do you believe in God?" It's like a simple true-false quiz: "God is a big critter living up there somewhere: Yes or no?" And that's really dumb.

So let's get straight from the beginning. God is not, and has never been, a critter or a "being" of any kind that would have weight or occupy space. That's Disney World, not religion. God is an idea, a concept. And theological questions are about the content and style of the concept and its relevance to life.

One of my favorite stories from any religious scripture is the ancient one in the Bible of Jacob wrestling with God. Technically, it wasn't God he was wrestling with, just a local deity guarding the river he wanted to cross. That's how we know what an ancient story this is—people used to believe that all boundaries were guarded by spirits, that to cross over, to grow beyond it, you had to wrestle with the god that guarded that boundary.

Modern psychologists know this to be true. To grow beyond a boundary that's kept us too small, too ignorant, too enslaved, we must be willing to wrestle. That's kind of what we're about here: wrestling with concepts of God that are unhealthy and small, that enslave rather than empower.

Still, it's a risky thing to do. In the Jacob story, he held on all night, finally receiving the blessing of the god and the ability to cross the river, and even getting a new name: Israel, the father of the Twelve Tribes. But he was wounded in the struggle and came out with a limp. He had that limp for the rest of his life. So it's risky.

I'm trying to do something hard as well as odd: I want to convince you that all gods are more like hand puppets than they are like puppeteers. Everyone who tells you what God is like or what God wants or says is using the concept like a hand puppet, creating or choosing which words his or her God can and cannot say. So whether it's a decent God or not usually depends on whose hands he's in.

I want to convince you that you know the difference between healthy concepts and bogus ones, and that only you can decide whether a god is good or bad, is worth serving with your life or not. I want to show you that the power is in you, not in the gods, and that you have known this, at some level, all along.

Here's what we already know: we wrestle with almost every authority claiming power over us. For instance, automakers routinely tell us their machines are perfectly safe. But both governmental and private firms are always testing them, always doubting that they're really telling us the truth, and are routinely exposing the design flaws the manufacturers were covering up. Why did they cover them up? Because it benefited them, even though it didn't benefit us. But we check it out, because lives are at stake.

Or think about pharmaceuticals. To pick just one, I remember when the manufacturers of Fen-Phen were on trial, how they insisted that the drugs were just effective weight-reducing aids with no serious side effects, that they had done extensive testing, that everyone was safe. But the FDA did independent tests and found that Fen-Phen damaged heart valves and could be fatal. Authoritative people lie. Even if they really believe what they're saying, we know they could be wrong. So we check it out, because lives are at stake.

These claims have three parts. Just knowing them can give you a kind of user's guide to hokum. Here is the three-step process by which truths and beliefs and gods are created. The first step is invisible. It has to be invisible for the game to work. The second step is that a company spokesman or some other authoritative figure tells us something is true. The third step is when they say that because it is true, we should go along with it, and everything will be all right.

But what all our investigations show is that there is a first step that they kept invisible. And the first step is that there is a set of facts or a state of affairs that would empower or enrich them, if it were really true. They have a stake in it; it's how they see the world.

So the whole three-step process goes like this: First, I want you to believe something because if you do, it will empower or enrich me, or will confirm my view of the world. Second, I convince myself, and then tell you, that this is true and good and safe. And third, since it is true and good and safe, you should follow it.

But when we want to know whether it's really true or good or safe, we check it out. You don't ask true believers to investigate their own truth-claims. You don't ask Ford executives whether the gas tanks on the company's Pintos are really safe. You don't ask the manufacturers of SUVs whether they have a high likelihood of tipping over and injuring or killing drivers and passengers. You don't ask the manager of a Jack-in-the-Box whether it's safe to eat his hamburgers. You ask a nonbeliever. An outsider. You ask someone who can tell the difference between fact and fiction, good and evil, and let them investigate.

We seem hardwired to respond to authoritative people and voices, so we are easy to fool. Advertising agencies, political advisors, and slick preachers all count on it. I'll tell you one more story that makes this point in a particularly enlightening way. You'll be able to spot all three steps, with the invisible first step last, in an exceptionally clear and dramatic form.

The story is one Joseph Campbell told about a tribe in Australia whose social order was maintained with the aid of bullroarers. These are long flat boards with a couple of slits cut in them and a rope tied to one end. They are swung around over one's head, producing an eerie, low kind of humming sound that seems quite otherworldly. When the gods were angry with the tribe, they would sound the bullroarers in the woods at night. No one, of course, ever saw them do this. The next day, the males of the tribe would explain what those gods were angry about and what behaviors had to change.

But the revelation comes at a key moment during the initiation of young men into manhood in the tribe. It's all very dramatic and very ritualized. In the evening, some of the tribe's men, wearing masks, come to kidnap the young boy. The women pretend to defend him, though they know the routine, and eventually the men overpower them and drag the boy into the woods.

Once there, the boy is tied to a table, and a frightening and bloody initiation rite takes place. Technically, it's called subincision, which means that, using a flint knife, a slit is made along the length of the underside of the boy's penis. (Men who have been through this have said that this makes them complete, with the genital marks of both a male and a female.)

But the revelation comes at the end. One of the men dips the end of the bullroarer in the boy's blood, brings it up near his face, then removes his mask—so the boy will recognize him as a man he's known all his life—and says the magical words: "We make the noises!" We make the noises we attribute to the gods. It's equally true everywhere; it's just seldom acknowledged as openly.

That's what our independent investigations of defective cars, infected hamburger, and deadly pharmaceuticals reveal, too. The authorities with the most to gain are the ones who make the noises saying we should believe them. And we have learned not to believe them until we have checked it out for ourselves. This is how concepts of gods are created.

There are thousands of examples from religion. To keep it manageable, I'll only take three, and just take them from the Hebrew Scriptures that are common to Judaism, Christianity, and Islam. All three of these come from the book of Deuteronomy, chapters 20 to 22. You can find dozens more like these in that book:

- "If a man is found lying with the wife of another man, both of them shall die" (22:22).
- "If upon marriage it is discovered that a woman isn't a virgin, the men of the city shall stone her to death" (22:20–21).
- "If a son is stubborn and won't obey his parents, then his parents will bring him to the elders at the city gate, and the men of the city will stone him to death" (21:18–21).

When you hear such things, you know that's a horrible concept of God that no decent or healthy person would admit into their lives. Even those Bible-waving preachers who insist that every word of the Bible is literally true never seem to quote these lines. They don't believe them either.

And we know it too, intuitively. You hear this ancient speaker claiming that these things are the word of God, and so you should obey them. But instinctively, you know better. Every parent of rebellious teenagers can understand the frustration in that last one. But every parent knows that anyone who actually did that, who actually had their own child murdered, would be a repugnant person following a repugnant god, not a god of life or truth or wholeness. You sense that these awful sayings must have originated in a particular time and place maybe 2,500 years ago, where whoever made them up was having trouble with authority or social control, so they put those bloody words in the mouth of their god, trying to give authority to them.

Only by doubting the authorities—in food production, car production, drug production, or god production—and trying to find out for ourselves what is good and what is evil, only by doing that can we ever escape from the fool's paradise of believing that all advertising companies, politicians, and preachers are trying to empower us rather than themselves.

So far, this sounds like a simple story of courage, of challenging authorities, defeating them, and exulting in triumph—like a bad martial-arts movie. But that's not all there is to it. Because every time we find another manufacturer's claims proven false, every time another group of politicians is caught lying to us, every time religious claims are shown to have been false and self-serving, we lose some of our naiveté and our trust.

That's the price of leaving paradise, the price of leaving Eden. Wrestling with gods usually leaves us with a limp. It's never a cheap victory. Remember when you stopped believing there was this one Santa Claus guy who came down every chimney bringing presents to every child every Christmas—even though you didn't have a chimney? Remember what you lost? Some people mark that as the end of their childhood innocence.

And what happens when you reconsider the concept of God? You look at whose hands God has been in, and suddenly God looks more like a hand puppet than a puppeteer. You investigate, and you realize God was never making the noises. People were making the noises: parents, preachers, politicians, people

21

with their own agenda for you. They made the noises they had been taught to make. Maybe they even believed them. But what happens when you realize they were not true?

If you take the liberal route, if you challenge and debunk those claims for truth or God, then in some ways the price is even steeper, and the limp even greater. For if even the idea of God you've been taught can be wrong, then what can't be wrong? How and where could you ever again find absolute certainty? And where, then, would you find your moral bearing?

You can lose faith in God. Do you also lose faith in even the idea of God? Many do. It's a limp. Do you lose faith even in the idea of truth, or goodness, justice, or beauty? That's worse than a limp. Don't do that.

You can always stay ignorant and not learn the difference. But the God in the Eden story was also created by priests and tribal chiefs who were served by that compliant ignorance. Why would you want to exalt them, or their self-serving idea of God? You might as well wrestle with God yourself, and cross over.

But crossing over, wrestling with God, isn't easy. For God is like Santa Claus in that way. You lost the child's magical Santa when your eyes were opened. And you lose the child's magical god in the same way—by having your eyes opened and realizing that we make the noises.

To wrestle with our gods is often to wind up disillusioned. I've had ministers tell me that's why they don't encourage their people to question the concept of God too deeply: they're afraid they'll become disillusioned. That sounds bad. But think about it: Is being disillusioned really worse than being "illusioned"? I'd think if you're "illusioned," you'd *want* to get disillusioned!

To wrestle with the concept of God and win, I think we need to be armed with a few reality-based facts:

- That we are made of stardust, we are deeply at home in the universe, intimately tied to everything, that the dynamic power of the universe is also in us, and that part of our destiny lies in reclaiming our noble origins.
- That all life on Earth is linked, too. We are not alone here; we are connected as members of a family. All people are our brothers and sisters. Here, in Iraq, in Nicaragua, everywhere.
- That authoritative claims that would take away our power and dignity and transfer them to others are usually lies: lies and blasphemies against life and truth and everything that is whole and holy.

Wrestling with the concept of God grants us both honor, and a task. Since we make the noises, it is now up to us to see that those noises are sacred noises: noises of truth that empower, not that enslave, truth that sets us free, not that puts us or others in heavier chains.

Part of growing up religiously is escaping from a child's Garden of Eden, understanding who makes the noises, and understanding that most of our truths and most of our gods are the hand puppets of the politicians, preachers, and churches. Those are false gods and need to be unmasked. But there is still wonder and miracle and mystery, and the magic of transformation in the world. We lose an excuse not to act. We lose an excuse for not getting involved. That's our human calling: to search for truth and wholeness east of Eden.

And what is left of the concept of God? Perhaps the Buddhists can help here. They tell the story of the finger pointing at the moon, and the poor people who spent all their time looking at the finger, never seeing the moon. Perhaps we shall gain a fresh view of the moon. And once we can see the light, that pointing finger is just a distraction, isn't it?

Good magicians don't reveal their tricks at the end of the show. But I'm not a magician; I'm a preacher, so I'll reveal mine here.

I hope you see that what I've tried to do here follows the same three steps I've been talking about. I start with what, to me, is the most true and useful way to understand how we make our gods. Then I've tried to persuade you that it's true, so you will adapt it for your own life.

Am I right? Is this the best kind of truth for you here? It's all I can offer you. From here, it's up to you. This is where I came out when I wrestled with the idea of God. Eventually, you'll need to wrestle, too. I recommend it. Even if the ordeal leaves you with a limp, it will bless you and might give you a new kind of name. After all, lives are at stake. And one of them may be yours.

3

Reality-Based Salvation

FEBRUARY 23, 2003

I've been thinking all week of the famous lines written almost sixty years ago by Pastor Martin Niemoller, after the fall of the Nazi movement in his Germany. He had been an outspoken critic of both Adolf Hitler and the Nazis almost from the start and ended the war in the concentration camp at Dachau, freed by the American army shortly before he was to be executed.

In 1945, he wrote this short confession, which has been quoted thousands of times:

> First they came for the Communists,
> and I didn't speak up,
> because I wasn't a Communist.
> Then they came for the Jews,
> and I didn't speak up,
> because I wasn't a Jew.
> Then they came for the Catholics,
> and I didn't speak up,
> because I was a Protestant.
> Then they came for me,
> and by that time there was no one
> left to speak up for me.

Niemoller's warning applies to religion as well as it does to politics. And the soul of his message is one Jesus put in even fewer words: We are all our brothers' and our sisters' keepers.

Since I didn't grow up in a conservative religion, most religious jargon isn't loaded for me. So I usually think of the word "God" as a symbol for our highest ideals and values. And I think of the word "salvation" in its original meaning: as health, wholeness (it comes from the Latin root for "to save," but also the root for "salve"). For me, the terms are kind of safe and abstract.

But when I hear many people's stories about why they left the churches of their childhood, or why their family avoided churches altogether, I realize that in the real world, "salvation" had a very different meaning, and not a very positive one. It meant getting a group's or a church's acceptance only as long as you agreed not to think outside the lines drawn by their orthodoxy. Neither my definition of God or of salvation would have worked in those churches. That's partly why I grew up unchurched: I didn't respect the few churches I tried.

I can't count the number of times I have heard people talk about how they felt when they knew they had to leave their old church. Some felt angry, some felt hurt, to realize that they couldn't stay because they didn't believe the church's orthodox teachings—they already sensed that the world just wasn't built that way—but it wasn't safe to say so out loud. Not that they'd be shot, but people would look at them funny if they had said they weren't so sure about this God stuff. They might have been called atheists or heretics. And they would have been made to feel uncomfortable, as though they weren't quite clean any more. So they left. It's also why so many people—a majority of U.S. citizens—neither attend nor trust churches. The gods are the hand puppets of those who speak for them, and salvation is your reward for going along with their game.

So I suppose what I really want to talk about here isn't salvation, but "the legitimate heir to what was once called" salvation. I love that phrase. It comes from my favorite philosopher, Ludwig

Wittgenstein (1889–1951), on whom I wrote my dissertation. When people finally understand him widely, it might change the nature of philosophy, and religion, in fundamental ways. At some point during his teaching years at Cambridge, other philosophers asked him what it was that he was doing: "It's certainly not philosophy!" they said. Wittgenstein's response was "Perhaps not, but it's the legitimate heir to what was once called philosophy." Now I want to talk for these few minutes about the legitimate heir to what was once called salvation.

There are two facets to salvation, and it's easy to emphasize the wrong one by thinking that all we have to do is just be honest and open about what we really believe, try to fashion beliefs that are true to both our heads and our hearts, then try to live them. But that's the easy part, the part we don't have to worry much about.

The second part of this salvation business—and the most important and most fragile part—is the thing Martin Niemoller was talking about. It is a kind of atmosphere within which it is safe to voice your beliefs, whether theological, social, moral, or political, without being made to feel that you are a second-class person, or a member of the damned. That atmosphere is what was lacking in whatever church you felt you had to leave. Why was it lacking? Because there are rules in all churches, and the church that offended you probably had the wrong rules.

In theological terms, these rules can be called orthodoxy: a set of beliefs endorsed by a group and used as the boundaries of permissible belief for everyone in the religion. Once orthodoxy is in place, the choices are closed, even if you hadn't finished choosing yet. And the theological word for choosing after some group has set up orthodoxy is *heresy*. When you look at it this way, heresy is the sacred thing, and orthodoxy is the blasphemy. Heresy is the Holy Spirit, alive and well, helping you find beliefs that can make you whole. Orthodoxy is a kind of groupthink that would cut you—and all the gods—down to the group's size.

The Greeks had a different image for orthodoxy in their story of Procrustes. He was this man with an iron bed. He was very friendly to his visitors, always offering them that bed to sleep on. But once on it, he forced them to fit into the bed by either stretching their bodies or cutting off their legs. He had his iron bed, and everyone had to fit it. That's orthodoxy.

Another image comes from the television series *Star Trek*. It's the group known collectively as the Borg. It is a kind of group, or cult, that simply assimilates everyone into it, erasing individual differences and essentially giving everyone the soul of the group.

And that word "cult" is another one referring to the biggest obstacle to finding your salvation in a church. Recently, I attended a lunch with Daniel McGuire, a Jesuit scholar brought to town by Planned Parenthood to talk about religious sanctions for both family planning and abortion.

During his luncheon talk, he referred to his church, the Catholic Church, as a cult. This shocked one Catholic woman there, who asked what he meant. A cult, he said, replaces your beliefs with its own. It assigns authority only to its own teachings, draws the boundaries on what is permissible to think, and excludes those who do not conform. In that sense, he said, the church has always been a cult, and an obstacle to salvation. And he pointed out what every religion student knows: that virtually all famous religious thinkers in history were heretics in their day, because they went beyond the beliefs accepted by their group. My favorite sound bite of the day came when McGuire defined conservatives as "worshipers of dead liberals."

I think all these images are good ones. So think of it as an orthodoxy, a Procrustean habit of cutting you down to fit someone else's bed, of the Borg absorbing your soul and giving you its own impersonal soul; or think of it as a cult that limits the acceptable beliefs. Whatever you call it, it is the mortal enemy of truth, the gods, and your ability to find salvation.

The most important facet of a quest for wholeness, authenticity, integrity, and salvation is the kind of atmosphere within which all sincere beliefs are equally welcome, equally "clean." Without that atmosphere, no community is finally safe.

I'm betting that people who left their church would not have left if their minister had been able to say, "Look, we're trying to explore what it means to be fully alive and human, as individuals, partners, parents, and citizens. Our tradition has had the habit of doing this in God-talk. But these are just ways of speaking. If you could put these common goals differently, please do. They're only ways of talking, after all, not sacred words. And the more ways we can say it, the more likely we really know what we're talking about."

That's the atmosphere I mean: the atmosphere or culture of the place that keeps all sincere opinions equally welcome. This doesn't mean you have to respect those opinions, understand! Opinions have to get their respect the old-fashioned way: they have to earn it, in open dialogue. And I'm not talking about frivolous, narcissistic, or sociopathic opinions—I'm remembering a church I knew where a disturbed member wanted to host a discussion group on the joys of pedophilia! But the people who hold sincere opinions have to feel welcome and "clean."

Too often, to find yourself and your beliefs, you have to leave the community that wants to cut you down to fit its iron bed. We've had a couple examples of this in Austin, both involving Baptist churches. Several years ago, the minister of University Baptist Church had a story about him on the front page of the *New York Times* because that church ordained a gay deacon, in violation of the new orthodoxy of the Southern Baptist Convention (SBC).

As a result, in order to live out their beliefs, they withdrew from the SBC.

And last year it happened again, when the First Baptist Church downtown withdrew from the SBC rather than conform to beliefs it felt were small and mean.

One of the least attractive things about human nature is our undying desire to make the world in the image of our beliefs: to turn our gods and our institutions into our hand puppets. If those beliefs are truly expansive and inclusive, that might be a good world. But they almost never are. They're almost always partisan, following the party lines of some theology, some social ideology, and some political platform. Iron beds. Iron beds, all.

Nearly all the great religious figures had to leave their communities to be saved, to find their distinctive wholeness and authenticity—Buddha, Jesus, Muhammad, all of them.

It can happen so easily. That expansive atmosphere is so very fragile, so easily destroyed. During graduate school, I attended an unusually liberal Christian church because it really did welcome all beliefs, and said so. It practiced an open communion. It was hard sometimes being clear about just where the boundaries were, whether anything could be presumed about all the members. Some of the more rigid Christians were always trying to bring back confessional tests of faith. Finally, someone suggested to the board that the church say that whatever beliefs people had, we could all agree that our primary purpose was to help establish the kingdom of God.

That was a metaphor for the best kind of world, the world with the most justice, fairness, and compassion. How could that metaphor be turned into something small and scary?

It didn't take long to find out. It was done by a man named Dan, a student preparing for the ministry. Dan was perhaps the most dedicated and courageous social activist I've ever met. He stood one Sunday during Prayers of the People and reminded us that Tuesday was Election Day and said, "You will either be working for or against the kingdom of God on Tuesday. If you vote Democratic, you are working for the kingdom of God. Otherwise, you are an enemy of God's kingdom. Remember that!"

Everyone was stunned. No one ever successfully confronted Dan, because he knew he was right, and right for the whole church. For my remaining three years there, the church was never quite the same. The next year a retired professor announced, during a week that he stood at the table for our monthly Communion, that Communion was a Christian sacrament, and as such was open to all Christians who had accepted Jesus Christ as their Lord and Savior. That really finished it. The fragile atmosphere was shattered, and no one knew how to repair it. Some of us just left and no longer had a church.

Later, I served a church where this liberal atmosphere necessary for the legitimate heir to salvation was shattered. There was a small group of secular humanists who were unhappy with a style of liberal religion, and finally, they got three of their group on the board, and one bullied the others into making him president of the board. Within months, he gave me a small piece of paper with a list of words I was not to use from the pulpit—words like "soul," "spirit," "God," and "miracle." He insisted that I still had freedom of the pulpit, but said those words offended the humanists, and my job as a minister was to care for their feelings, so to be an adequate minister I couldn't use those words.

Of course, I did use those words. An increasingly vicious fight went on for over two years. They were so sure they were right that one of them finally made a public death threat against me, in front of a board member and the church administrator. I preached the second service that morning while police were outside taking statements.

The most dangerous people on earth are those who think there is only one right position, which just happens to be theirs. These people are found in religion's orthodoxies and cults, in political systems that claim the right to arrest dissenters, or in other social, theological, or cultural ideologies that work like the Borg.

The reason it is so easy for us to recognize images like Procrustes' iron bed, cults, or the Borg is because all these come from something deep within our human nature—dangerous, but absolutely natural. We would all be most comfortable in a world where we got to prescribe some basic beliefs and values for others, just as our gods become the hand puppets of those who speak for them. We create orthodoxies at the drop of a hat: theological, political, social—even down to dress codes.

Salvation is like democracy—only eternal vigilance can make it possible. So here you are. You may wonder what you need to do to make American society a place that can allow room for the legitimate heir to salvation. Remember, salvation has two parts. The first is that you have to bring your own questions, your own beliefs, and be willing to work on them until they feel adequate to live by, and then keep working on them as long as you want to keep growing.

But the other one, the maintenance of that fragile atmosphere within which all sincere beliefs are equally welcome and equally "clean"—that's where you owe something here. That's where you owe your own vigilance, to counter that unquenchable desire we all have to subtly trim the acceptable beliefs to fit the bed in which we've grown so comfortable.

If the legitimate heir to salvation can be found in churches at all, it is only available in healthy liberal churches. And they are only healthy if that invisible, fragile, life-giving atmosphere is preserved, within which all sincere religious, political, or moral beliefs are equally welcomed into dialogue in a community of moral equals who will ultimately never agree on the best way to be saved.

And what is it? How else can it be put? I think there is something about this "legitimate heir to what was once called salvation" that is more advanced and challenging than the mere notion of salvation, even in its traditional liberal interpretations (health, wholeness, integrity, authenticity, and so on).

It goes beyond mere salvation to say that even more important than our own growth is our duty—our sacred duty—to preserve and maintain that fragile liberal atmosphere within which all may freely pursue their different paths to the kind of wholeness we call salvation. The Buddhists speak of the *sangha*, or sacred community, as one of the essential parts of the path to enlightenment. Some very few might do it alone, but most of us need to be part of a community of seekers, people who know to regard ultimate concerns as ultimate rather than secondary, as society does. Our spiritual roots grow deep and our branches reach high only in serious soil, in a "garden" kept safe by the mutual protection of all in the community who know—as Martin Niemoller learned the hard way—that finally none can be free or safe unless all are free and safe. This is true not only of churches, but also—and much more importantly—of societies.

There is an ancient image for the understanding of "truth" that underlies this picture: it's the old story of the blind people and the elephant. The "elephant" is life, in all its complexity and mystery. Each "blind person" is one person, or even one discipline (psychology, geology, theology, history, and so on.). They can see only what the deep biases of their discipline (or their personal biography) permit. No one will ever see the whole "elephant." And even if it were possible to see every possible view, and understand all disciplines with something to say about life and the human condition, it would still be paltry. In terms of the metaphor, you can't understand an elephant unless you *are* the elephant—and even then, you'd be only one "elephant"; there are so many more.

The legitimate heir to what was once called salvation exists in a pluralistic world where humility is part of the whole intellectual and spiritual enterprise and where, because of this, all sincere beliefs, investigations, perspectives, and feelings must be allowed into the never-ending open discussions about life's ultimate concerns. And they cannot be welcome unless we in the spiritual community, the *sangha*, covenant to protect and defend that essential, life-giving, fragile atmosphere within which all sincere people and opinions are welcomed into both discussion and fellowship.

If I understand the teachings of Jesus right, he would have called this the kingdom of God. Buddha might have called it a community of the enlightened who recognize the Buddha-seeds in all others, and who protect and nurture those precious seeds.

Joseph Campbell once said that an authentic person rejuvenates the world. Imagine what an authentic society might do.

The fact that your political or religious beliefs don't work for me should be all the proof I need that mine aren't likely to work for you. It sounds, and is, a bit messy. But that's the mess of people trusted with their freedom. Where all sincere beliefs are equally welcomed into dialogue, we can find—if not salvation, then the legitimate heir to what was once called salvation. In fact, it is the only kind of place where we *can* find it.

PART TWO

FASCISM

4

The Fundamentalist Agenda

FEBRUARY 3, 2002

The most famous definition of fundamentalism is probably still some variation on H. L. Mencken's assessment of Puritanism as "the haunting fear that someone, somewhere may be happy." There's something to this. It's too fearful, too restrictive, too lacking in faith to provide a home for the human spirit to soar or for human societies to blossom.

But there isn't enough to it. An adequate understanding of fundamentalism contains some inescapable and uncomfortable critiques of America's cultural liberalism of the past four decades. We were given the rare chance of a revelation in the aftermath of the attacks on September 11, 2001. That revelation came in two stages.

First was a list of things some Muslim fundamentalists hate about our culture:

- They hate liberated women, and all that symbolizes them. They hate it when women compete with men in the workplace, when they decide when or whether they will become breeders, when they show the independence of getting abortions, and when laws are changed that previously gave men more power over them.
- They hate the wide range of sexual orientations and lifestyles that have always characterized human societies. They hate homosexuality, can't confront the homosexual

tendencies that exist in them, and so project them outward
and punish them in others.
- They hate individual freedoms and rights that allow
people to stray from the single, rigid sort of truth with
which they want to constrain all people.

Not much about these revelations was really new. We saw all
this before, when Khomeini's Muslim fundamentalists wreaked
such havoc in Iran in the years following 1979, or when the
Taliban took control of Afghanistan in the mid 1990s.

But the surprise came two days after September 11, in that
remarkably unguarded interview on *The 700 Club* between Jerry
Falwell and Pat Robertson. It was remarkable partly because
these men are so media savvy it's amazing they would say such
things on the air. But it's also remarkable because as they listed
the "causes" of the September 11 attacks, we heard exactly the
same hate list the Afghan Taliban had outlined:

- They hate liberated women who don't follow orders,
who get abortions when they want them, who threaten,
or laugh at, their arrogant pretensions to rule them.
- They hate the wide range of sexual orientations that have
always characterized human societies. They would force
the country to conform to a fantasy image of two married
heterosexual parents where the husband works and the wife
stays home with the children—even when that describes
less than one-sixth of current American families.
- They hate individual freedoms that let people stray from
the one simple set of truths they want imposed on all in
our country. Pat Robertson has been on record for a long
time saying that democracy isn't a fit form of government
unless it is run by fundamentalist Christians of his kind.

It is terribly important for us to realize that the fact that "our" Christian fundamentalists have the same hate list as "their" Muslim fundamentalists is not a coincidence!

From 1988 to 1993, the University of Chicago conducted a six-year study known as "The Fundamentalism Project," the largest such study ever done. About 150 scholars from all over the world took part, reporting on every imaginable kind of fundamentalism. And what they discovered was that the agenda of all fundamentalist movements in the world is nearly identical, regardless of religion or culture.

They identified five points shared by virtually all fundamentalisms:

1. Their rules must be made to apply to all people, and to all areas of life. There can be no separation of church and state, or of public and private areas of life. The rigid rules of God—and they never doubt that they and only they have got these right—must become the law of the land. Pat Robertson, again, has said that just as Supreme Court justices place a hand on the Bible and swear to uphold the Constitution, so they should also place a hand on the Constitution and swear to uphold the Bible.

2. Men are on top. In every way. Men are bigger and stronger, and they rule not only through physical strength, but also and more importantly through their influence on the laws and rules of the land. Men set the boundaries, men define the norms, and men enforce them. They also define women, and they define them through narrowly conceived biological functions. Women are to be supportive wives, mothers, and homemakers.

3. Since there is only one right picture of the world, one right set of beliefs, and one right set of roles for men,

women, and children, it is imperative that this picture and these norms and rules be communicated precisely to the next generation. Therefore, they must control the education of the society. They control the textbooks, the teaching styles, and they decide what may and may not be taught.

4. There is an amazingly strong and deep resemblance between fundamentalism and fascism. Both have almost identical agendas. One scholar suggested that it's helpful to understand fundamentalism as religious fascism, and fascism as political fundamentalism. Fundamentalists spurn the modern and want to return to a nostalgic vision of a golden age that never really existed. Likewise, the phrase "overcoming the modern" is a fascist slogan dating back to at least 1941.

5. Fundamentalists deny history in a radical and idiosyncratic way. Fundamentalists know, as well or better than anybody, that culture taints everything it touches. Our teachers and our times color how we think, what we value, and the kind of people we become. If you have perverse teachers or books, you develop perverse people and societies. And they agree on the perversions of our current American society: the air of permissiveness, narcissism, and individual rights unbalanced by responsibilities; sex divorced from commitment; and so on. What they don't want to see is that exactly the same thing was true when their own sacred scriptures were written. Good biblical scholarship begins by studying the cultural situation when scriptures were created, to understand their original intent so we can better discern what messages they may still have that are relevant for our lives. But if fundamentalists admit that their own

scriptures are as culturally conditioned as everything else, they lose the foundation of their certainties. Saint Paul had severe personal hang-ups about sex, for instance, that lie behind his personal problems with homosexuality and women. How else would he say that it is a shameful thing for a woman to speak in church, or that men are made in the image of God, but women are made in the image of men? These are the reasons that informed biblical scholars take some of Paul's teachings as rantings, not revelations. But for fundamentalists, their scriptures fell straight from heaven in a leather-bound book, every jot and tittle intact.

Now something should be bothering you about this list. And that's that except for the illustrations I've added, you can't tell what religion, culture, or even century I'm talking about! This realization also stopped the scholars a dozen years ago while they were presenting abstracts of their papers at the fall meetings in Chicago. Several of them noted that all their papers were sounding alike, that they were reporting on "species" and needed to be studying the "genus," that there were strong family resemblances between all these fundamentalisms, even when the religions had had no contact, no way to influence each other.

This is one of the most important things we need to learn about the agendas of all fundamentalisms in the world. They are all alike. *And the only way that can be the case is if the agenda preceded all the religions.*

And it did. These behaviors are familiar because we've all heard and seen them many times. These men are acting the role of alpha males who define the boundaries of their group's territory and the norms and behaviors of their in-group. These are the behaviors of tens of thousands of territorial species in which males are stronger than females. Or to put it into jargon, these are the characteristic behaviors of sexually dimorphous territorial animals. Males set and enforce the rules; females obey the males and raise the children.

What the conservatives are conserving is the biological default setting of our species—virtually identical with the default setting of ten thousand other species. This means that when fundamentalists say they are obeying the word of God, they have severely *understated* the authority for their position. The real authority behind this behavioral scheme is tens of millions of years older than all the religions and all the gods there have ever been. It is the picture of life that gave birth to most of the gods, as its projected protectors.

It's absolutely natural, ancient, powerful—and completely inadequate. It's a means of structuring relationships that evolved when we lived in troops of 150 or fewer. But in the modern world, it's completely incapable of the nuance or flexibility needed to structure human societies in humane ways. But it does help us better understand the relative roles of conservatives and liberals in modern society, and the role that liberals play in giving birth to fundamentalist uprisings.

The conservative impulse that has its starkest form in the fundamentalist agenda is our attempt to give stability to our societies. And as many observers have noted, hierarchical structures tend to be very stable.

The liberal impulses serve to give us not stability but civility—or humanity. The primary job of liberals is to enlarge our in-group. This is the plot of virtually all liberal advances in society. Giving women the vote eighty years ago was expanding the in-group from only adult males to include adult females. Once that larger definition was established by liberals, conservatives began defending that definition of the in-group rather than the smaller one.

Likewise, the civil rights movement was a way of saying that our in-group was multicolored. Every liberal advance adds to the list of those who belong within our society's protected group.

This means that, while society is a kind of slow dance between the conservative and liberal impulses, the liberal role is the more important one. It provides civility and humanity; it makes our societies humane rather than just stable and mean.

It also means that in order for the liberal impulse to lead, liberals must remain in touch with the moral center of our territorial nature. Fundamentalist uprisings are an early warning system telling us that the liberals have failed to provide an adequate and balanced vision, that they have not found a vision that attracts enough people to become stable.

Just as it's no coincidence that all fundamentalisms have similar agendas, it's also no coincidence that the most successful liberal advances tend to be made by liberals wrapping their expanded definitions in what sound like extremely conservative categories.

John F. Kennedy's most famous line sounds like the terrifying dictate of the world's worst fascism: "Ask not what your country can do for you; ask rather what you can do for your country." Imagine that line coming from Hitler, Khomeini, the Taliban, or Pat Robertson and Jerry Falwell! It could be a conservative, even a fascist, slogan. Yet Kennedy used it to effect significant liberal transformations in our society. Under that umbrella, he created the Peace Corps and Vista and enlisted many young people to extend their hand to those they had not before seen as belonging to their in-group—liberal ends achieved through what sounded like conservative means.

Likewise, the Reverend Martin Luther King used the rhetoric of a conservative vision, expanded through his liberal redefinition of the members of our in-group. When he defined all Americans as the children of God, those words could well be the battle cry of an American Taliban on the verge of putting a Bible in every school, a catechism in every legislature. Instead, King used that cry to include Americans of all colors in the sacred and protected group of "all God's children"—which was just what many Southerners were arguing against forty years ago. Liberal ends, conservative means.

When liberal visions work, it's because they have kept one foot solidly in the moral center of our deep territorial impulses, and the other free to push for a bigger tent, to expand the definition of those who belong in "our" territory.

And when liberal visions fail, it is often because they fall short of achieving just this kind of balance between our conservative impulses and our liberal needs.

During the past half century, many of our liberal visions have been too narrow, too self-absorbed, too unbalanced. And their imbalance has been a key factor in triggering the fundamentalist uprisings of the past decades. And when society doesn't follow liberal visions, liberals haven't led well (or at all).

When liberals burned the American flag during the Vietnam War rather than waving it and insisting that America live up to its great tradition, they lost the most powerful symbol in our culture and the ability to speak for our national interests. This created an imbalance that planted the seeds of future fundamentalist uprisings.

When liberals defined abortion in amoral terms, as simply a matter of individual rights—where only the mother, but not the developing baby, were "individuals"—they created a moral imbalance and planted the seeds of future fundamentalist uprisings (while quietly losing the support of many liberals, including liberal ministers).

When liberals overemphasized individual rights while ignoring the need to balance them with individual responsibilities toward the larger society, they planted the seeds of future fundamentalist uprisings.

Those uprisings are happening in some Muslim societies that hate us and hate the influence our culture is having on their own. They are also threatening our own culture, as shown by that amazing interview on *The 700 Club* and some of both Robertson's and Falwell's statements of the past two decades.

But if I'm right in what I'm suggesting here, it isn't their fault. The fundamentalists are reacting absolutely instinctively— whether they think they have instincts or not—to a threat to social stability made up of the narrow and unbalanced liberal teachings of the past three or four decades.

Maintaining both stability and civility, humane content and enduring form, is an unending dance between the conservative and the liberal impulses within our societies. But the task of liberals is much, much harder.

It's really quite easy to be a fundamentalist. All you have to do is cling tightly to a few simplistic teachings too small to do justice to the complex demands of the real world. You just have to cling to these, and then pretend that what you have done is either honest or noble.

But to be a liberal, really to be an awake, aware, responsive, and responsible liberal—that can take, and make, a whole life.

5

The Dark God of Capitalism

OCTOBER 8, 2000

I want to talk with you about capitalism and economics—not as an economist, but as a theologian.

I know very little about economics. I'm not a CPA and couldn't begin to analyze complicated financial pictures. But I am a theologian, and I do know something about gods. I know how they work, how powerful they are, how invisible they usually are, and I know that beneath nearly every human endeavor with any passion or commitment about it there will be a god operating, doing the things gods do.

Gods are those central concerns that our behaviors show we take very seriously. We commit our lives to them, we are driven by them, and in return they promise us something we want, or think we want. Whether what they promise us is good or bad is a measure of whether the god involved is an adequate or an inadequate one.

The Greeks have a wonderful picture of the seduction of, and the consequence of, following idols. It's in Homer's *Odyssey*, on Odysseus's return home. Just before he comes to the Straits of Messina, he has his famous encounter with the Sirens, the seductive goddesses who lured sailors to their deaths. Their sweet voices promised a life of love, ecstasy, ease, and all-round wonderfulness that was just too good to be true. When you looked on the beaches of their island, you saw nothing but the bleached bones of the fools who had followed them: they *were* too good to be true.

Odysseus, you may remember, wanted to have the experience and feel the temptation, but was wise enough to know that no mortal can long resist the Sirens. So he had his men tie him to the mast, making them swear they would not untie him no matter what he may say. Then they put beeswax in their own ears and sailed past the Sirens. The Sirens were so persuasive that Odysseus screamed at his men to untie him, so he might sail toward them. But they couldn't hear him. So in spite of his momentary wishes—you might say—Odysseus lived to serve nobler causes.

As a theologian, I'd say that the most important fact we can know about ourselves is to know the gods we're serving in our lives and in our societies, and whether they are really worth our lives. And in this age of skepticism and disbelief, one of the biggest misunderstandings about us is that we have no gods, that we're not a religious people.

I'm interested in this battle between gods and idols, and how that is being played out in our economy today. It isn't a simple thing, the contrast between people and profits. Its roots go all the way back to our Founding Fathers, over two hundred years ago, who had very mixed opinions of "we the people"—many of them pretty insulting. Alexander Hamilton declared that the people are "a great beast" that must be tamed. Rebellious and independent farmers had to be taught, sometimes by force, that the ideals of the revolutionary pamphlets were not to be taken too seriously.

Or as John Jay, the first chief justice of the Supreme Court, put it, "The people who own the country ought to govern it." James Madison stated that the primary responsibility of government is "to protect the minority of the opulent against the majority." Those "without property, or the hope of acquiring it, cannot be expected to sympathize sufficiently with its rights," Madison explained.

This sounds like today's cynical capitalism, but it was not. Like Adam Smith and the other founders of classical liberalism, Madison was precapitalist, and anticapitalist in spirit. But education, philosophical understanding, and gentility were associated with money. I don't think they would see that connection between money and character to be as strong today, when many of our very worst people are rich.

Still, Madison hoped that the rulers in this "opulent minority" would be "enlightened Statesmen" and "benevolent philosophers," whose "wisdom may best discern the true interests of their country." He soon learned differently, as the "opulent minority" proceeded to use its power much as Adam Smith had predicted it would a few years earlier. By 1792, Madison warned that the rising developing capitalist state was "substituting the motive of private interest in place of public duty," leading to "a real domination by the few under [a merely] apparent liberty of the many."

The battle between democracy and private profit making has been a continuous thread in American history since the country began. A century ago, the American philosopher John Dewey was still writing, in the same key as Jefferson and Madison had, that democracy has little content when big business rules the life of the country through its control of "the means of production, exchange, publicity, transportation and communication, reinforced by command of the press, press agents and other means of publicity and propaganda." Dewey wrote this in the days before radio, television, or mass media. He also wrote that in a free and democratic society, workers must be "the masters of their own industrial fate," not tools rented by employers.

It is a little eerie how much John Dewey sounds like James Madison, when Madison wrote that "a popular Government, without popular information, or the means of acquiring it, is but a Prologue to a Farce or a Tragedy; or perhaps both."

So there are these two powerful and opposite ideas in our society, both with roots going all the way back to our founding as a nation. Both centers of thinking are still battling to be the gods—or idols—that define us, our hopes and possibilities, our society. Will the people rule the country, or will big businesses rule the country and the people?

We live in a time when the scales have tipped heavily toward capitalism and away from democracy.

How did that happen? One obvious culprit—or hero, depending on your perspective here—is the great economist Milton Friedman, who said, in his influential book *Capitalism and Freedom*, that profit making is the essence of democracy, so any government that pursues antimarket policies is being antidemocratic, no matter how much informed popular support they might enjoy. That's a powerful, terrifying, revolutionary redefinition of democracy.

But once you place profits over people, the manipulation of us masses becomes a constant part of the scheme. Clearly, people don't want to do more work for less money, to lose their power, their possibilities, even their chance of realistic hope, and so the art of deceiving us has been with us a long time, too.

But it is not a secret art. Since the 1920s until recently, it was talked about quite openly. One of the most important names in the art of bamboozling the masses was Edward Bernays, who worked in President Woodrow Wilson's Committee on Public Information, the first U.S. state propaganda agency. Bernays wrote that "[i]t was the astounding success of propaganda during the [First World] war that opened the eyes of the intelligent few in all departments of life to the possibilities of regimenting the public mind."

Here are more words from this most influential American: "The conscious and intelligent manipulation of the organized habits and opinions of the masses is an important element in democratic society." To carry out this essential task, "the intelligent minorities must make use of propaganda continuously and systematically" because they alone "understand the mental processes and social patterns of the masses," and can "pull the wires which control the public mind." This process of "engineering consent"—a phrase Bernays coined—is the very "essence of the democratic process," he wrote, shortly before he was honored for his contributions by the American Psychological Association in 1949.

Another member of Wilson's propaganda committee was Walter Lippmann, one of the most influential and respected journalists in America, and a brilliant, articulate man. The intelligent minority, Lippmann explained in essays on democracy, is a "specialized class" that is responsible for setting policy and for "the formation of a sound public opinion." It must be free from interference by the general public, who are "ignorant and meddlesome outsiders." The public must "be put in its place"; their function is to be "spectators of action," not participants—apart from periodic electoral exercises when they choose among the specialized class.

About a trillion dollars a year are now spent on marketing. Much of that money is tax deductible, producing the irony that we are paying many of the costs of the manipulation of our attitudes and behavior. But that's just domestic news. And capitalism, like all gods, is a jealous god and knows no national boundaries. Eventually, most gods and idols want to rule the world.

When the North Atlantic Free Trade Agreement (NAFTA) legislation for Canada, the United States, and Mexico was rushed through Congress—despite 60 percent public opinion against it—contradictory studies were suppressed or ignored. The Office of Technology Assessment, for instance, which is the research bureau of Congress, published a report saying that NAFTA would harm most of the population of North America.

What NAFTA made possible on an international scale was the ability of corporations to increase profits for the owners by disempowering and dismissing their workers, who are terrified that the owners will take the business to Mexico, Saipan, Burma, Vietnam, and other cheap-labor and forced-labor markets, which is what they are doing. We have become a little numb to the fact that when the stock market rises, it almost always means that tens of thousands of our neighbors have been fired, their benefits or insurance cut or eliminated, and work is being done by dollar-a-day workers in other countries, often under inhumane conditions. This is capitalism working as it was designed to work.

After all the positive hype to push the passage of NAFTA through, we don't hear much about the post-NAFTA collapse of the Mexican economy, exempting only the very rich and U.S. investors (protected by U.S. government bailouts). Mexico was successfully transformed into a cheap-labor market with wages only one-tenth of U.S. wages, driving people farther down into poverty, while their American counterparts lost their jobs. Wages here have fallen to the level of the 1960s for production and nonsupervisory workers. The Congressional Office of Technology Assessment predicted that NAFTA "could further lock the United States into a low-wage, low-productivity future." But that report, like a lot of others, was suppressed or ignored.

You don't have to ask who won. This is capitalism. The people who control the capital won. Nobody else.

The quality of our economy, according to the pundits on television, is determined by the stock market. Yet again, we must ask what small part of the economy we're talking about. Half the stocks in 1997 were owned by the wealthiest 1 percent of households, and almost 90 percent were owned by the wealthiest 10 percent. The figures are worse if you look at bonds and trusts. Today's upper-class prosperity is built almost entirely on the bloated prices of corporate stocks.

While the number of Americans getting college degrees is increasing, there are some who feel that this is a cynical ploy to make the degrees more worthless, because the real growing job market looks to be low tech and low paid. Between now and 2006, according to the Bureau of Labor Statistics, among the thirty fastest-growing job categories, only seven require even a bachelor's degree. More than half of them pay under $18,000 a year. Moreover, 25 percent of the jobs in today's celebrated economy pay a poverty wage. That's 32 million people. Farmers today get only 20¢ of the food dollar you and I spend, a nickel less than just a decade ago. That's a 20 percent drop in income, in just one decade.

If you back off to think of this battle of the rights of profits versus people, you could imagine, at least theoretically, an extreme kind of world in which the rights of corporations—which, incidentally, should have no rights at all, only the privilege of existing as long as the public believes they are serving the general good— could actually trump the rights of people, states, even nations. Imagine a world in which corporations could sue nations if those nations took actions that cost the corporations revenues. In other words, imagine that a nation decided a gasoline additive was toxic to the environment and banned gasoline containing the additive, and that nation was then sued by the corporation for loss of revenues. Or imagine a case where a corporation went into another country, used its power to create an illegal monopoly driving local firms out of business. Let's say the locals caught on, took the corporation to court, and the court ruled against the corporation and even fined it for illegal business practices. It could happen. But in this most bizarre of imaginary worlds, imagine that the corporation could then sue the entire nation for loss of profits.

And imagine, since we've already crossed over into the insane, that the corporation could bypass all the courts in the nation it was suing and win a multimillion-dollar judgment against a country decided by a three-person team of financial advisors, of which the corporation got to pick one.

No need to imagine any of that. It is now very real, courtesy of chapter eleven of NAFTA.

For instance, the Loewen Group, a large funeral-home conglomerate in Canada, was successfully sued by the owner of a local funeral parlor in Biloxi, Mississippi, for unlawful practices aimed at driving local parlors out of business, and a jury issued a $260-million judgment against Loewen, which was then further raised to $400 million. But then, Loewen invoked chapter eleven of NAFTA and went to a three-person "corporate court," saying the rights of its investors had been harmed, and chapter eleven allows the corporation to recoup its losses from the U.S. government. Loewen is seeking $750 million from the U.S. government; the case is pending. In another case, the Ethyl Corporation, based in Virginia, sued the Canadian government for banning its leaded gasoline and labeling its additive toxic (our own EPA is working to ban the same toxic additive). Canada was sued for $251 million; the little panel of trade arbiters met with government officials and settled for having the government pay the company $13 million and apologize for implying that their gasoline additive is dangerous. By doing this, they have set a precedent for corporations being able to sue governments for loss of profit and for denying people and whole nations the right to protect their people and their environment from poisonous chemicals added to their fuel or food, as long as some corporation is making a profit from it.

Remember Thomas Jefferson's prescient statement from two centuries ago: "The selfish spirit of commerce knows no country, and feels no passion or principle but that of gain." The spirit of capitalism is a lot like the spirit of the Sirens, promising what they cannot deliver, but doing it so very seductively. What is happening is what Thomas Jefferson and many of the other founders of this country feared would happen. The power has shifted from the people to the corporations, and laws are being enacted and enforced that let profits trump people and international corporations trump nations. This is the logic under which the media and politicians of both major parties can define ours as a "strong" economy while wages for most Americans are lower in constant dollars than they were thirty years ago, personal bankruptcy rates set new records every year, we have the highest child poverty rate in the developed world, the highest mortality rate for children under five in all the industrial nations, and Americans in their twenties are the first generation not expected to do better financially than their parents. If this is a "strong" economy, we need to ask for whom, and at whose expense.

This is a betrayal of democracy barely short of treason.

Capitalism is doing very well. It is serving the needs of those who control the capital above all other needs, as it is supposed to do. Our economy, despite the raving stories, is not doing well. But our problems are not primarily economic. They're religious. We're worshiping false gods. For the past generation in this society, our social and political policies have been increasingly dictated by the overriding concerns of capitalism.

It's all happened before. We've always been so seduced by the glitter of gold that we're on the verge of making it into a god. There's nothing new here. Once money is turned into a god, it is—like all deities—a jealous god and will not permit any other consideration to come before it. So we sell the righteous for silver and Vietnamese girls for a pair of Nike tennis shoes.

When we exalt capitalism as we have, when we change tax

structures and income distribution to create, as we have, the greatest disparity between rich and poor since the Middle Ages, I can see, and feel, that our problems aren't about money. They're theological. We are worshiping idols again, and unless we stop it, everything else will follow inexorably from that—as it always has.

Note: A lot of the material for this sermon came from Noam Chomsky's book, *Profits over People*, and Jim Hightower's book, *If the Gods Had Meant for Us to Vote, They Would Have Given Us Candidates*. Other books I read in preparation for the sermon included *How to Overthrow the Government*, by Arianna Huffington; *Rich Media, Poor Democracy*, by Robert McChesney; *Republic of Denial*, by Michael Janeway; and *Amusing Ourselves to Death*, as well as *How to Watch TV News*, by Neil Postman.

6

The Corporation Will Eat Your Soul

APRIL 25, 2004

You may have heard the story of the frog and the scorpion. A scorpion wanted to cross a swift river and asked a frog to carry him on his back. "How do I know that you won't sting and kill me as soon as you get on my back?" asked the frog.

"Well," answered the scorpion, "then I wouldn't be able to get across the river."

"Then how do I know that you won't sting and kill me as soon as we're across the river?"

"Oh," said the scorpion, "because I'll be so grateful for the ride, why would I want to kill you then?"

This convinced the frog, so he let the scorpion on his back, and began crossing the river. They were about two-thirds of the way across the raging river, when, to his great surprise, the frog felt a painful sting and looked around to see the scorpion pulling his stinger out of the frog's back. Very soon, the frog felt himself becoming numb. Just before he was completely paralyzed, the frog asked why.

"It's just my nature," said the scorpion, as they both sank into the river and drowned. "It's just my nature."

Of course, the story was never really about scorpions. It was meant as a warning against certain rare but dangerous kinds of people whose nature, like that of scorpions, is to destroy others even if it destroys them at the same time. One of the scariest things we can imagine is a machinelike thing with a will that seeks to harm us and feels nothing when we suffer or die. Think of those androids in the *Matrix* movies, for instance; or the Orcs and Sauron in *Lord of the Rings*.

I suppose the most famous story like this is still Mary Shelley's 1818 tale of Dr. Frankenstein and the monster he created from spare parts. For nearly two centuries, the Frankenstein monster has been a symbol of creating something inhuman, giving it life and immense power without a soul, then living to see it turn on us, as the monster even killed Frankenstein in the end.

When I was growing up, the most powerful movie like this was the original 1956 version of *Invasion of the Body Snatchers*. For me, it was a movie about the difference between real people and pathological people. You probably know the story. A mindless life force from outer space drifted from a desolate, dead planet and wound up on this one. It operated under a simple program. When a human fell asleep near one of these odd pods, the pod produced a duplicate of the sleeping person: an exact duplicate of body and memory. The life was drained from the human and infused into the copy. You could hardly tell the difference. These faux humans looked the same, had all the same memories. But they had no soul. They had no compassion, no feeling for anyone. The squeals of a dog getting killed by a car in the road twenty feet away didn't even make them care to look. Life didn't matter to them, only reproducing their kind; they had no other end than reproducing their kind. Eventually, like the scorpion, they killed everything. Then if the cosmic winds were right, this mindless life force might blow across the galaxy and suck the life out of yet another planet.

When humans act like this, we think there's something fundamentally wrong with them. Theologians call them evil, writers call them monsters or body snatchers, and psychologists call them psychopaths. Since *psyche* means "soul," the word really means people with sick souls. Here's a list of psychopathic traits I recently came across: irresponsible; grandiose and self-absorbed; lacking empathy; not accepting responsibility for destructive actions; unable to feel remorse; all power, no depth; all manipulation, no connection.

Now what is this about? Why am I talking about persons who are not real persons, psychopaths and scorpions whose nature is to destroy, even if it also destroys them?

It's a way of introducing the powers that have largely taken over American society and are on the verge of taking over the world. But I am talking about something that we have created, a person that is not a real person, that has immense power, more money than God, and that, like the invasion of the body snatchers, is seeking to, and succeeding in, destroying the compassionate qualities of both societies and real people.

You'll think I've badly overstated the case when I say that this dangerous person who is not a real person is the corporation. So let me try and persuade you.

Joel Bakan, the author of *The Corporation: The Pathological Pursuit of Profit and Power,* explains the nature, the character, and the danger of large corporations, which were formed in the late seventeenth and early eighteenth centuries, to pool the money of a large number of people in order to give them more power than any single person or business could have. Very early, laws were passed saying investors had no real liability for whatever dastardly deeds the corporation did. This gave the corporation limited liability, but unlimited ability to make money.

And from the start, as a matter of structure and law, the only purpose of a corporation was to make as much money as possible for its stockholders.

By the late nineteenth century, the courts had transformed the corporation into a person, a legal person, and even spoke of it in that way. And in 1866, lawyers representing this newly created "person" won a ruling from the Supreme Court saying that, as a legal person, corporations were covered under the "due process of law" and the "equal protection of the laws" granted by the Fourteenth Amendment. These provisions were written for the protection of freed slaves after the Civil War. But since 1866, it has almost never been used by freed slaves and almost exclusively been used by corporations—even when they make slaves of workers all over the Third World and, some would argue, within our own country. I am betting that not many of you knew that. Until a few years ago, I didn't know it either. Isn't that odd, that we didn't know that?

Since being christened as persons, corporations have not been seen as evil. They're just doing business as usual. It's just their nature.

And what are their aims? If a corporation sells stocks, its sole legal purpose, under U.S. laws, is to make as much money as possible for its stockholders. The corporation can pretend to care about society or the environment, as long as the money it spends makes more people want to buy its products and increase profits for stockholders. But it may not, legally, spend money for social good unless it is aimed at increasing profits.

Milton Friedman calls making money the corporation's only moral aim. He compares little acts of apparent social conscience to car manufacturers using pretty girls to sell cars. "That's never really about the girls," he points out. "It's just a trick to sell cars." Likewise, a corporation can donate to the Special Olympics or civic projects, but only if it will help sell more of its product. A corporation cannot do social good for the sake of doing social good.

Peter Drucker, perhaps the oldest living guru of corporate character, says if you have a CEO who wants to do social good, fire him fast! And there are laws supporting this perspective. Ninety years ago, when Henry Ford was becoming astoundingly rich from selling his Model T Fords, he decided that he was making too much money. So in 1916, as Bakan writes in his book, Ford "cancelled the stock dividends to give customers price reductions because he felt it was wrong to make obscene profits." Soon, two of his major investors, the Dodge brothers, took him to court, arguing that profits belonged to the stockholders, not the company, and the court agreed with them, establishing a precedent that still rules. Corporations exist as persons only to do whatever is necessary to maximize profits for their stockholders, even if it harms people. (Yes, the Dodge brothers then started their own car company.)

In a 1933 Supreme Court judgment, Justice Louis Brandeis finally made the obvious connection, when he stated that corporations were "Frankenstein monsters" capable of doing evil.

Bakan cites another famous case from 1994, in which General Motors was sued because on Christmas Day 1993 a mother with her four children in the car was hit from behind while stopped at a stop light, causing the gas tank of her 1979 Chevy Malibu to explode, burning and badly disfiguring all five of them. During the trial, an internal GM report from an analyst was introduced showing that management knew the gas tank was set so far back that it could explode on impact, killing the car's occupants. In fact, about five hundred people a year were being killed this way at the time of the report in 1973 when the new Malibu style cars were being planned. The report said that each fatality would cost GM $200,000 in legal damages, and then divided the figure by 41 million, the number of cars GM had on the road, and concluded that the financial cost to GM was only $2.40 per automobile. The cost of ensuring that fuel tanks did not explode in crashes was estimated to be $8.59 per car. That meant the company could save $6.19 per car if it let people die in fuel-fed fires rather than alter the design of vehicles to avoid such fires.

While the jury handed out a huge award, it was later reduced by three-quarters, and GM appealed the case. In support of GM, the U.S. Chamber of Commerce filed a brief defending the practice of using this kind of "cost-benefit analysis in corporate decision making." The jury's decision, they said, was deeply troubling, because manufacturers should use cost-benefit analysis to make the most profitable decisions. The corporation's legal makeup, its nature, requires executives to make only those decisions that create greater benefits than costs for their stockholders. Executives have no authority to consider what harmful effects a decision might have on other people or upon the environment, unless those effects might have negative consequences for the corporation.

Do you see what has happened here? This "person" we created through our own laws, by following its legal nature, can and does endanger and kill human beings in the pursuit of profit.

Now let's jump to a very different area of society, one you might not think is even related to corporations. It's the subject of our armed forces, what they are really serving and what our soldiers are really dying for. Bakan's book tells of a chapter in American history I was never taught in school. It involves a Marine Corps general named Smedley Butler, one of World War One's most heavily decorated soldiers. On August 21, 1931, Butler had stunned an audience at an American Legion convention in Connecticut when he had said:

> I spent 33 years . . . being a high-class muscle man for
> Big Business, for Wall Street and the bankers. In short, I
> was a racketeer for capitalism. . . . I helped purify Nica-
> ragua for the international banking house of Brown

Brothers in 1909–1912. I helped make Mexico and especially Tampico safe for American oil interests in 1916. I brought light to the Dominican Republic for American sugar interests in 1916. I helped make Haiti and Cuba a decent place for the National City [Bank] boys to collect revenue in. I helped in the rape of half a dozen Central American republics for the benefit of Wall Street. . . .

In China in 1927 I helped see to it that Standard Oil went its way unmolested. . . . I had . . . a swell racket. I was rewarded with honors, medals, promotions. . . . I might have given Al Capone a few hints. The best he could do was to operate a racket in three cities. The Marines operated on three continents.

Given that speech, and Butler's disgust with the role the military played in serving the greed of large corporations, what happened three years later is truly stunning. Franklin Roosevelt was president, and he was bringing government regulations in to stop the disastrous greed of the wealthiest corporations and individuals. Big business hated him. On August 22, 1934, General Butler was approached in a hotel room in Philadelphia by a messenger for a group of wealthy businessmen, who opened a large suitcase of $1,000 bills and dumped it on the bed, explaining that this was only a down payment. The business interests wanted General Butler to assemble a volunteer army, take over the White House, and install himself as the fascist dictator of the United States, with the financial support of big business. Some observers believe that if they had picked a different general, it may well have worked. Butler refused and told the story.

In 1934, the business interests believed they would have to use military force to take over the government, dismantle democracy, and install a form of fascist government doing the will of the

richest corporations and individuals in America, to the degrada-
tion or destruction of everyone else. This was the invasion of the
body snatchers, coming closer than we can know to succeeding.

"Today, seventy years after the failed coup, a well-organized
minority again threatens democracy," writes Bakan. "Corporate
America's long and patient campaign to gain control of government over the last few decades, much quieter and ultimately
more effective than the plotters' clumsy attempts, is now succeeding. Without bloodshed, armies, or fascist strongmen, and using
dollars rather than bullets, corporations are now poised to win
what the plotters so desperately wanted: freedom from democratic control."

And their reach is now worldwide. The World Trade Organization, which President Bill Clinton created in 1993, has already
sued or threatened to sue nations, including ours, for safety or
environmental laws that cut into a corporation's profits. In 2005,
their full power will come into effect, enabling them to prevent
governments from enacting environmental or health regulations
that would unduly impede their profits.

NAFTA, another Clinton creation, was an investor-protection
plan enabling corporations to use cheap labor to force American
wages down, break unions, and steal jobs from U.S. workers by
the hundreds of thousands, "outsourcing" them to cheap-labor
markets around the world in order to let rich corporations and
individuals get richer.

Is there hope? Can anything be done? Yes, but only if we
remember that we created this Frankenstein monster, and it is
only a "person" because we said so, and we can change our views
and change our laws and change the way in which corporations
are allowed to do business in this country and in the world.

And New York attorney general Eliot Spitzer recently said that
if "a corporation is convicted of repeated felonies that harm or

endanger the lives of human beings or destroy our environment, the corporation should be put to death, its corporate existence ended, and its assets taken and sold at public auction." Spitzer isn't antigovernment. He works for the government. The government isn't bad; it's a neutral but powerful tool that can be used to reclaim our nation and redefine the acceptable role of corporations in our world. We created corporations, we defined them, and we have the authority to redefine them, to insist that they may only operate in our society if they are organized to serve the greater good of the majority in our society, rather than simply the arrogant greed of a tiny percentage of us. They need to be taxed to pay a fair share of our economy's expenses, just as the tax rates on rich individuals need to be raised. In 1960, the tax rate was 91 percent for the richest Americans, and corporations paid fair taxes. That is why our middle class was empowered after World War Two, because the money was being distributed fairly. Today, we have socialism for the rich, and a brutal kind of capitalism for everyone else. We can stop it.

And now we're at war again, a war General Butler would recognize immediately. Halliburton, the company from which Vice President Cheney came back to Washington, has made billions of dollars from no-bid contracts. Other large U.S. corporations that contributed to the presidential campaign have also made hundreds of millions of dollars. Some of their civilian truck drivers in Iraq are being paid $80,000 a year to risk getting killed making profits for the stockholders. Meanwhile, many of our American soldiers, as you may have read, are getting paid $16,000 a year, a pay so low that they are being given food stamps with their pay, and many of their families back home are on welfare. The soldiers are not fighting and dying for democracy, freedom, or anything noble at all. They are dying, like General Butler's soldiers died eighty years ago, as inconsequential drones whose only purpose in life is to help Halliburton and other major U.S. corporations and rich individuals make a lot of money. If they get killed, at least they're cheap to replace. There's cost-benefit analysis at work.

This is the story of the Frankenstein monster come full circle, to the point where it is succeeding in forcing its human creators to serve it, even if they become beggars or corpses by doing so. It is un-American. It is ungodly. It is inhuman, and it is disgusting. And it is continuing. Only the American people are likely to stop it, and then only if they wake up, get informed, get angry, get organized, and get going.

I can't write an ending for this sermon. It would have to be written in the real world, in real time, by real people. But there is something riding on our backs that doesn't belong there, and that does not have our best interests at heart. It will, if it is allowed to remain there, eat our soul and our society. Nor can it really stop itself. It's just its nature.

> Note: Most of the information I used for this sermon came from a remarkable new book called *The Corporation: The Pathological Pursuit of Profit and Power* by a Canadian law professor named Joel Bakan, published by the Free Press in 2004.

7

Oil, Arrogance, and War

I want to try and make sense of our coming wars, to put them
into a pattern that might create more light than heat—though
some heat, too. I think the patterns and the plans are now clear
enough. I read the former attorney general Ramsey Clark's
powerful letter to the secretary general of the United Nations,
in which he said that President Bush came into office determined to attack Iraq and change its government. Clark is saying,
as others have said, that the Bush administration is not making it
up as it goes along, but following a plan.

In some ways, we've known about this plan since his father
was president. Then, it was called the "New World Order."
The *Sunday Herald* of Glasgow, Scotland, recently published a
story about an important sketch of the military dimensions of
this plan, where details are spelled out and very little reading
between the lines is needed. I read the eighty-page paper entitled *Rebuilding America's Defenses: Strategy, Forces and Resources for
a New Century, a Report of the Project for the New American Century*
(www.newamericancentury.org) that was published in September 2000, before President Bush took office. Let's consider some
excerpts: "At present the U.S. faces no global rival. America's
grand strategy should aim to preserve and extend this advan-
tageous position as far into the future as possible. . . . [This]
requires a globally preeminent military capability both today
and in the future. . . . [The goal of all this is to maintain] a global

security order that is uniquely friendly to *American principles and prosperity* . . . an international security environment conducive to *American interests and ideals* . . . [that protects] *American interests and principles*" [emphasis added].

We need to translate the italicized terms, because they're not straightforward. "American principles" does not refer to democratically elected governments in these countries. We have routinely helped dictators who cooperated with our economic ambitions gain power, including the Shah of Iran, Mobutu Sese Seko in the Republic of Congo, Augusto Pinochet in Chile, all of whom replaced democratically elected heads of government.

"In broad terms," the authors of the report write, "we saw the project as building upon the defense strategy outlined by the Cheney Defense Department in the waning days of the Bush Administration."

Among other things, it proposes that the military must have the ability to "fight and decisively win multiple, simultaneous major theater wars," and that the United States cannot "assume a . . . stance of neutrality; the preponderance of American power is so great and its global interests so wide that it cannot pretend to be indifferent to the political outcome in the Balkans, the Persian Gulf or even when it deploys forces in Africa. Finally, these missions demand forces basically configured for combat. . . . American troops, in particular, must be regarded as part of an overwhelmingly powerful force."

In the Middle East, the report says "the need for a substantial American force presence in the Gulf transcends the issue of the regime of Saddam Hussein. . . . American armed forces stationed abroad and on rotational deployments around the world . . . are the cavalry on the new American frontier."

In addition to land forces, the report talks at some length about the need to command and control both space and cyberspace.

The vast majority of military information, here and abroad, is received from commercial space satellites. We need to be able to deny access to these satellites to all we consider enemies. Likewise, we need to protect our computer systems from hacking, viruses, and so on, while developing methods of invading and infecting the computer systems of our enemies.

This report is about plans for military forces sufficient to seize control of entire economies now that we are the lone superpower. Yet it speaks of war almost as a video game, or an action movie, in which none of the "good guys" would ever die. This is the aspect that has made some critics call these people "chicken hawks." They—including Bush, Cheney, and many others on Bush's staff—dodged the draft when it was their turn, but have a passionate, almost rhapsodic, love for the idea of war. I found one extended passage in this report, talking about the future of war, which is illustrative of this worldview:

> Although it may take several decades for the process of transformation to unfold, in time, the art of warfare on air, land, and sea will be vastly different than it is today, and "combat" likely will take place in new dimensions: in space, "cyberspace," and perhaps the world of microbes. Air warfare may no longer be fought by pilots manning tactical fighter aircraft sweeping the skies of opposing fighters, but a regime dominated by long-range, stealthy unmanned craft. On land, the clash of massive, combined-arms armored forces may be replaced by the dashes of much lighter, stealthier and information-intensive forces, augmented by fleets of robots, some small enough to fit in soldiers' pockets. Control of the sea could be largely determined not by fleets of surface combatants and aircraft carriers, but from land- and space-based systems,

forcing navies to maneuver and fight underwater. Space itself will become a theater of war, as nations gain access to space capabilities and come to rely on them. . . . And advanced forms of biological warfare that can "target" specific genotypes may transform biological warfare from the realm of terror to a politically useful tool.

Future soldiers may operate in encapsulated, climate-controlled, powered fighting suits, laced with sensors, and boasting chameleon-like "active" camouflage. "Skin-patch" pharmaceuticals help regulate fears, focus concentration and enhance endurance and strength. A display mounted on a soldier's helmet permits a comprehensive view of the battlefield—in effect to look around corners and over hills—and allows the soldier to access the entire combat information and intelligence system while filtering incoming data to prevent overload.

This is merely a glimpse of the possibilities inherent in the process of transformation. . . . Until the process of transformation is treated as an enduring military mission—worthy of a constant allocation of dollars and forces—it will remain stillborn.

The paper also notes that "the process of transformation, even if it brings revolutionary change, is likely to be a long one, absent some catastrophic and catalyzing event—like a new Pearl Harbor."

That's the gist of their military plan, with its sorrowful note that it will take a long time unless there were some catastrophic and catalyzing event. Let's look at the economic plan, to see whom it is designed to benefit and who is left out.

Since about 1980, the American economy has shifted money, power, and possibilities from the lower 60 or 80 percent of our citizens to the top few percent. As Kevin Powers notes in his book *Wealth and Democracy*, from 1981 to 1986, the income tax on America's wealthiest people was reduced from 70 percent to 28 percent. Twenty years earlier, it had been 91 percent. During the decade of the 1980s, the portion of our nation's wealth held by the top 1 percent nearly doubled, from 22 percent to 39 percent, probably the most rapid escalation in U.S. history. Taxes on corporations have fallen as dramatically; some large corporations now pay almost nothing in taxes.

This isn't an economic plan to separate the upper and lower classes—it is much more specific and restricted. It is a plan that will separate the top 1 percent from all below them.

During the past twenty years, we have heard some cynical, or comical, talk about "trickle-down economics." But as many have noted and tens of millions have experienced, almost nothing that trickles down is fit to consume. Among the Western industrialized nations, we have the highest percentage of poverty among those over the age of sixty-five, the highest level of child poverty, the largest gap between richest and poorest, the lowest percentage graduating from high school, and the highest youth homicide rate.

Yet the economic disparities in the United States are nothing compared with the conditions in Iraq, where, as Ramsey Clark pointed out, our sanctions have cost the lives of five hundred Iraqi citizens for every one of our citizens killed on 9/11. It doesn't compare to other poor economies being exploited by our corporations: the Asian workforce of young women making our tennis shoes for a total wage of about $500 a year, or the situation in areas of China where the average wage is only 39¢ an hour, yet our Wal-Mart Corporation negotiated work contracts to make their goods at only 13¢ an hour.

The last time the American economy was this badly out of

balance was in the post–World War One years leading up to the crash of 1929. And eighty-one years before 9/11, in September 1920, terrorists—American terrorists—exploded dynamite outside the offices of financier J. P. Morgan, killing thirty-four and wounding over two hundred. That too was an attack on symbols of economic abuse, not a declaration of war on America.

And that is also why our World Trade Center and Pentagon buildings were attacked on September 11, 2001. It was not an attack on "America" any more than the bombing in 1920 was.

Spinmeisters have played bad word games here, by identifying "America" as the victim of the 9/11 attacks. No, the victims were the nearly 3,000 innocent citizens who happened to work in highly symbolic buildings. America's role was as the country whose long-term economic and military arrogance prompted the murderous actions of the terrorists—crimes for which those responsible should be brought to international justice.

What the terrorists didn't understand, however, was that the attacks of 9/11 became the "catastrophic and cataclysmic event" that would provide the Bush administration with an excuse to try and push through the aggressive military takeover of world markets and world freedoms. What happened on 9/11 was the "Pearl Harbor" event that would permit rapid transformation of our society and the military expansion needed to establish the New World Order.

Still, Pearl Harbor wasn't really the right historical precedent for 9/11 and its aftermath. That precedent, as many have noted, was the Reichstag fire of 1933. Please understand that I will not compare our president with Hitler. But I will compare, as others have, the tactics both administrations used to transform a terrorist attack into a means of taking authoritarian control of their citizens.

On January 30, 1933, Adolph Hitler was appointed chancellor of Germany, though his party did not have a majority in the parliament. Four weeks later, on February 27, the government building—the Reichstag—was burned in Berlin. Hitler immediately declared it was an attack on Germany by the Communists, and arrested 4,000 Communists that night. The next day, President Hindenburg and Hitler suspended virtually all civil liberties in the name of national emergency. A supplemental decree created the SA (Storm Troops) and SS (Special Security) federal police agencies.

Within the next few days, 40,000 of Hitler's political opponents were arrested, marking the end of democracy and the rise of fascism in Germany. The rest, as we know, is history.

It mustn't seem coincidental that individual rights were the first things restricted by both the Nazis in 1933 and our government after September 2001. The New World Order is a command-and-control empire, in which those to be commanded must first be disempowered. Nor may we believe it's a coincidence that the Homeland Security Force resembles the SS, in its sole allegiance to the leader, with no protection for whistle-blowers. Our rights must be removed for the same reason that this New World Order requires massive military might all over the world: because no free people would allow themselves to be controlled in this way for the benefit of so very few.

Here's another way to define the New World Order: it is "a system of government that exercises a dictatorship of the extreme right, typically through the merging of state and business leadership, together with belligerent nationalism"—that is the definition given in the 1983 *American Heritage Dictionary* for fascism.

Articles are appearing in this and other countries showing a U.S. lust for control of Iraq's estimated 112-billion-barrel oil reserves as key motives for attacking Iraq. In a September 15, 2002, article in the *Washington Post* entitled "In Iraqi War Scenario, Oil Is Key Issue: U.S. Drillers Eye Huge Petroleum Pool," the paper reported that the United States was using Iraq's oil as a "bargaining chip" to get the backing for tough actions against Iraq from Russia, Britain, China, and France, all of whom, along with the United States, form the United Nations Security Council. Here is an excerpt from that article:

> "It's pretty straightforward," said former CIA director R. James Woolsey, who has been one of the leading advocates of forcing Hussein from power. "France and Russia have oil companies and interests in Iraq. They should be told that if they are of assistance in moving Iraq toward decent government, we'll do the best we can to ensure that the new government and American companies work closely with them."
>
> But he added: "If they throw in their lot with Saddam, it will be difficult to the point of impossible to persuade the new Iraqi government to work with them."

Since George Bush proclaimed his "war on terror," other countries have claimed the right to strike first. India and Pakistan brought the earth and their own people closer to nuclear conflict than ever before as a direct consequence of claims by the United States of the unrestricted right to pursue and kill terrorists, or attack nations protecting them, based on a unilateral decision without consulting the United Nations. There is already a near epidemic of nations proclaiming the right to attack other nations or intensify violations of human rights of their own people on the basis of George Bush's assertions.

And as Ramsey Clark pointed out, Bush's "war on terror" is being used as a diversionary tactic to save a failing presidency that has converted a healthy economy and treasury surplus into trillion-dollar losses; to fulfill the dream, which will become a nightmare, of a New World Order to serve special interests in the United States; to settle a family grudge against Iraq; to weaken the Arab world, one people at a time; to strike a Muslim nation to weaken Islam; and to secure control of Iraq's oil to enrich U.S. interests, further dominate oil production in the region, and control oil prices.

Beyond that, the "war on terror" is also diverting attention from the stunning fact that in just one year, President Bush has squandered the immense amount of goodwill extended to the United States after 9/11.

Meanwhile, tens or hundreds of thousands of the world's innocent civilians will be slaughtered for these dreams of economic and military control. And tens of thousands of our own soldiers will be killed, disfigured, or scarred for life to serve, not freedom or democracy, but arrogance, greed, and a fantasy of world domination that is simply insane.

I hesitate to quote from Al Gore's speech, but found one part compelling: "If what America represents to the world is leadership in a commonwealth of equals, then our friends are legion; if what we represent to the world is empire, then it is our enemies who will be legion."

If and when this doomsday scenario unfolds, thoughts and sermons like this will be seen as un-American.

But they are not un-American. They are among the most patriotic, intelligent, and sane responses we can make to these Dr. Strangelove–like plans for world domination that are on the verge of plunging us into unimaginable terror, a war debt of perhaps a billion dollars a day that will drain our Social Security reserves and worsen the gap between the richest and the rest. In the long run, it will also mark Americans for generations to come as a malevolent people, lacking both healthy principles and principled courage.

True patriotism is the demand that great nations follow only great ideals. True Americans will fight to keep this great nation from squandering the hopes of the many on the mad furies of the few. And true religious faith must demand that as a nation we become agents of compassion, not conflagration.

It was faith and patriotism of this high caliber that inspired the best of our nation's founders. And it will only be the courage to return to these higher and more commanding ideals that might still rescue us at this late hour.

8

Living under Fascism

NOVEMBER 7, 2004

You may wonder why anyone would try to use the word "fascism" in a serious discussion of where America is today. It sounds like cheap name-calling, or a melodramatic allusion to a slew of old war movies. But I am serious. I don't mean it as name-calling at all. I mean to persuade you that the style of governing into which America has slid is most accurately described as fascism, and that the necessary implications of this fact are rightly regarded as terrifying. And even if I don't persuade you, I hope to raise the level of your thinking about who and where we are now, to add some nuance and perhaps some useful insights.

The word comes from the Latin word *fasces*, denoting a bundle of sticks tied together. The individual sticks represented citizens, and the bundle represented the state. The message of this metaphor was that it was the bundle that was significant, not the individual sticks. If it sounds un-American, it's worth noting that the Roman fasces appear on the wall behind the Speaker's podium in the chamber of the U.S. House of Representatives. It's true that America chose the bundled sticks or arrows to symbolize our motto of *E Pluribus Unum* ("Out of Many, One") rather than from any fascist leanings. But today, the symbol makes a very different kind of sense from its original intent.

Still, it's an unlikely word. When most people hear the word "fascism" they may think of the racism and anti-Semitism of Mussolini and Hitler. It is true that the use of force and the scapegoating of fringe groups are part of every kind of fascism. But there was also an economic dimension of fascism, known in Europe during the 1920s and 1930s as "corporatism," which was an essential ingredient of Mussolini's and Hitler's tyrannies. So-called corporatism was adopted in Italy and Germany during the 1930s and was held up as a model by quite a few intellectuals and policy makers in the United States and Europe.

As I mentioned earlier (in "The Corporation Will Eat Your Soul"), *Fortune* magazine ran a cover story on Mussolini in 1934, praising his fascism for its ability to break unions, disempower workers, and transfer huge sums of money to those who controlled the money rather than those who earned it.

Few Americans are aware of, or can recall, how so many Americans and Europeans viewed economic fascism as the wave of the future during the 1930s. Yet reviewing our past may help shed light on our present and point the way to a better future. So I want to begin by looking back to the last time fascism posed a serious threat to America.

In Sinclair Lewis's 1935 novel *It Can't Happen Here*, a conservative Southern politician is helped to the presidency by a nationally syndicated radio talk show host. The politician—Buzz Windrip—runs his campaign on family values, the flag, and patriotism. Windrip and the talk show host portray advocates of traditional American democracy—those concerned with individual rights and freedoms—as anti-American. That was sixty-nine years ago.

One of the most outspoken American fascists from the 1930s was economist Lawrence Dennis. In his 1936 book *The Coming American Fascism*—a coming that he anticipated and cheered—Dennis declared that defenders of "18th-Century Americanism" were sure to become "the laughing stock of their own countrymen." The big stumbling block to the development of economic fascism, Dennis bemoaned, was "liberal norms of law or Constitutional guarantees of private rights."

So it is important for us to recognize that, as an economic system, fascism was widely accepted in the 1920s and 1930s and nearly worshiped by some powerful American industrialists. And fascism has always, and explicitly, been opposed to liberalism of all kinds.

Mussolini, who helped define modern fascism, viewed liberal ideas as the enemy. "The Fascist conception of life," he wrote, "stresses the importance of the State and accepts the individual only in so far as his interests coincide with the State. It is opposed to classical liberalism [which] denied the State in the name of the individual; Fascism reasserts the rights of the State as expressing the real essence of the individual."

Mussolini thought it was unnatural for a government to protect individual rights. The essence of fascism, he believed, is that government should be the master, not the servant, of the people.

Still, "fascism" is a word that is completely foreign to most of us. We need to know what it is, and how we can know it when we see it.

In an essay coyly titled "Fascism Anyone?" Dr. Lawrence Britt, a political scientist, identifies social and political agendas common to fascist regimes. His comparisons of Hitler, Mussolini, Franco, Suharto, and Pinochet yielded this list of fourteen "identifying characteristics of fascism." See if they sound familiar.

1. *Powerful and continuing nationalism.* Fascist regimes tend to make constant use of patriotic mottos, slogans, symbols, songs, and other paraphernalia. Flags are seen everywhere, as are flag symbols on clothing and in public displays.

2. *Disdain for the recognition of human rights.* Because of fear

of enemies and the need for security, the people in fascist regimes are persuaded that human rights can be ignored in certain cases because of "need." The people tend to look the other way or even approve of torture, summary executions, assassinations, long incarcerations of prisoners, and so on.

3. *Identification of enemies/scapegoats as a unifying cause.* The people are rallied into a unifying patriotic frenzy over the need to eliminate a perceived common threat or foe: racial, ethnic, or religious minorities; liberals; communists; socialists; terrorists; and so on.

4. *Supremacy of the military.* Even when there are widespread domestic problems, the military is given a disproportionate amount of government funding, and the domestic agenda is neglected. Soldiers and military service are glamorized.

5. *Rampant sexism.* The governments of fascist nations tend to be almost exclusively male dominated. Under fascist regimes, traditional gender roles are made more rigid. Opposition to abortion is high, as are homophobia and antigay legislation [in] national policy.

6. *Controlled mass media.* Sometimes the media are directly controlled by the government, but in other cases, the media are indirectly controlled by government regulation, or sympathetic media spokespeople, and executives. Censorship, especially in wartime, is very common.

7. *Obsession with national security.* Fear is used as a motivational tool by the government over the masses.

8. *Religion and government are intertwined.* Governments in fascist nations tend to use the most common religion in the nation as a tool to manipulate public opinion. Religious rhetoric and terminology is common from

government leaders, even when the major tenets of the religion are diametrically opposed to the government's policies or actions.

9. *Corporate power is protected.* The industrial and business aristocracies of a fascist nation often are the ones who put the government leaders into power, creating a mutually beneficial business–government relationship and power elite.

10. *Labor power is suppressed.* Because the organizing power of labor is the only real threat to a fascist government, labor unions are either eliminated entirely, or are severely suppressed.

11. *Disdain for intellectuals and the arts.* Fascist nations tend to promote and tolerate open hostility to higher education and academia. It is not uncommon for professors and other academics to be censored or even arrested. Free expression in the arts is openly attacked, and governments often refuse to fund the arts.

12. *Obsession with crime and punishment.* Under fascist regimes, the police are given almost limitless power to enforce laws. The people are often willing to overlook police abuses and even forego civil liberties in the name of patriotism. There is often a national police force with virtually unlimited power in fascist nations.

13. *Rampant cronyism and corruption.* Fascist regimes almost always are governed by groups of friends and associates who appoint each other to government positions and use governmental power and authority to protect their friends from accountability. It is not uncommon in fascist regimes for national resources and even treasures to be appropriated or even stolen outright by government leaders.

14. *Fraudulent elections.* Sometimes elections in fascist nations are a complete sham. Other times elections are manipulated by smear campaigns against, or even assassination of, opposition candidates, use of legislation to control voting numbers or political-district boundaries, and manipulation of the media. Fascist nations also typically use their judiciaries to manipulate or control elections.

This list will be familiar to students of political science. But it should be familiar to students of religion as well, for much of it mirrors the social and political agenda of religious fundamentalisms worldwide. It is both accurate and helpful for us to understand fundamentalism as religious fascism, and fascism as political fundamentalism. They both come from very primitive parts of us that have always been the default setting of our species: amity toward our in-group; enmity toward out-groups; hierarchical deference to alpha-male figures; a powerful identification with our territory; and so forth. It is that brutal default setting that all civilizations have tried to raise us above, but it is always a fragile thing, civilization, and has to be achieved over and over and over again.

Still, this is not America's first encounter with fascism.

In early 1944, the *New York Times* asked Vice President Henry Wallace to, as Wallace noted, "write a piece answering the following questions: What is a fascist? How many fascists have we? How dangerous are they?" Wallace's answer to those questions was published in the *Times* on April 9, 1944, at the height of the war against the Axis powers of Germany and Japan. See how much you think his statements apply to our society today: "The really dangerous American fascist," Wallace wrote, ". . . is the man who wants to do in the United States in an American way what Hitler did in Germany in a Prussian way. The American fascist would prefer not to use violence. His method is to poison the channels of public information. With a fascist the problem is never how best to present the truth to the public but how best to use the news to deceive the public into giving the fascist and his group more money or more power."

In his strongest indictment of the tide of fascism he saw rising in America, Wallace added, "They claim to be super-patriots, but they would destroy every liberty guaranteed by the Constitution. They demand free enterprise, but are the spokesmen for monopoly and vested interest. Their final objective toward which all their deceit is directed is to capture political power so that, using the power of the state and the power of the market simultaneously, they may keep the common man in eternal subjection."

By these standards, a few of today's weapons for keeping the common people in eternal subjection include NAFTA, the World Trade Organization, union busting, cutting worker benefits while increasing CEO pay, elimination of worker pensions, rapacious credit-card interest rates, and outsourcing of jobs—not to mention the largest prison system in the world.

Our current descent into fascism came about through a kind of "perfect storm," a confluence of three unrelated but mutually supportive schools of thought.

The first major component of this perfect storm has been the desire of very wealthy Americans and corporate CEOs for a plutocracy that will favor profits for the very rich and disempowerment of the vast majority of American workers, the destruction of workers' unions, and the alliance of government to help achieve these greedy goals. It is a condition some have called socialism for the rich, capitalism for the poor, and that others recognize as a reincarnation of Social Darwinism. This strain of thought has been present throughout American history. Seventy years ago, in 1934, a handful of very wealthy business leaders tried to finance a military coup to replace Franklin Delano Roosevelt and establish General Smedley Butler as a fascist dictator. Fortunately, they picked a general who really was a patriot; he refused, reported the scheme, and spoke and wrote about it. As Canadian law professor Joel Bakan wrote in the book (and documentary) *The Corporation*, our plutocrats have now achieved their coup without firing a shot.

Our plutocrats have had no particular interest in religion. Their global interests are with an imperialist empire, and their domestic goals are in undoing all the New Deal reforms of Franklin Delano Roosevelt that enabled the rise of America's middle class after World War Two.

The second stream of thought was the imperialistic dream of the Project for the New American Century (PNAC, www .newamericancentury.org). I don't believe anyone can understand the past four years without reading the PNAC report, published in September 2000 and authored by many who have been prominent players in the Bush administrations, including Vice President Dick Cheney, Secretary of Defense Donald Rumsfeld, as well as Paul Wolfowitz, Richard Perle, and Donald Kagan, to name only a few. The authors of this report saw the fall of Communism as a call for America to become the military ruler of the world, to establish a new worldwide empire. They spelled out the military enhancements we would need, and then noted, sadly, that these wonderful plans would take a long time, unless there could be a catastrophic and catalyzing event like a new Pearl Harbor that would let the leaders turn America into a militarist country. There was no particular interest in religion in this report, and no concern with local economic policies.

The third powerful stream must be credited to Pat Robertson and his Christian Reconstructionists, or Dominionists. Long dismissed by most of us as a screwball, Robertson has been preaching the Dominionist style of Christianity since the early

1980s and is now the most powerful religious voice in the Bush administration.

Katherine Yurica, who transcribed over 1,300 pages of interviews from Robertson's *The 700 Club* shows in the 1980s, has shown how Robertson and his chosen guests consistently, openly, and passionately argued that America must become a theocracy under the control of Christian Dominionists. Robertson is on record saying democracy is a terrible form of government unless it is run by his kind of Christians. He also rails constantly against taxing the rich, against public education, social programs, and welfare—and prefers Deuteronomy 28 over the teachings of Jesus. He is clear that women must remain homebound as obedient servants of men, and that abortion, like homosexuals, should be made illegal. Robertson has also been clear that other kinds of Christians, including Episcopalians and Presbyterians, are enemies of Christ.

Another ill wind in this perfect storm is more important than its crudity might suggest: it was President Bill Clinton's sleazy sex with a young but eager intern in the White House. This incident, and Clinton's equally sleazy lying about it, focused the certainties of conservatives on the fact that "liberals" had neither moral compass nor moral concern, and therefore represented a dangerous threat to the moral fiber of America. While the effects of this may be hard to quantify, I think they were profound.

These "storm" components have no necessary connection, and come from different groups of thinkers, many of whom wouldn't even like one another. But together, they form a nearly complete web of command and control, which has finally gained control of America and, they hope, of the world.

When all fascisms exhibit the same social and political agendas, then it is not hard to predict where a new fascist uprising will lead. The actions of fascists and the social and political effects of fascism and fundamentalism are clear and sobering. Here is some of what we can expect to happen in our country in the next few years:

- The theft of all Social Security funds, to be transferred to those who control money, and the increasing destitution of all those dependent on Social Security and social-welfare programs.
- Rising numbers of uninsured people in this country, which already has the highest percentage of citizens without health insurance in the developed world.
- Increased loss of funding for public education, combined with increased support for school vouchers, urging Americans to entrust their children's education to Christian schools.
- More restrictions on civil liberties as America is turned into the police state necessary for fascism to work.
- Withdrawal of virtually all government funding for the Public Broadcasting System. At their best, these media sometimes (though seldom) encourage critical questioning, so they are correctly seen as enemies of the state's official stories.
- The reinstatement of a draft, from which the children of privileged parents will again be mostly exempt, leaving our poorest children to fight and die in wars of imperialism and greed that could never benefit them anyway.
- More imperialistic invasions—of Iran and other places—and the construction of permanent military bases and a huge embassy in Iraq.
- More restrictions on speech, under the flag of national security.
- Control of the Internet to remove or cripple it as an instrument of free communication that is exempt from

government control. This will be presented as a necessary antiterrorist measure.

- Efforts to remove the tax-exempt status of liberal churches and to characterize them as anti-American.
- Tighter control of almost all media and demonization of the few media that they are unable to control—the *New York Times*, for instance.
- Continued outsourcing of jobs, including more white-collar jobs, to produce greater profits for those who control the money and direct the society, while simultaneously reducing America's workers to a more desperate and powerless status.
- Moves in the banking industry to make it impossible for an increasing number of Americans to own their homes. As they did in the 1930s, those who control the money know that it is to their advantage and profit to keep others renting rather than owning.
- Criminalization of those who protest as un-American, with arrests, detentions, and harassment increasing. We already have a higher percentage of our citizens in prison than any other country in the world. That percentage will increase.

In the near future, it will be illegal or at least dangerous to say the things I have said here. In the fascist story, these things are un-American. In the real history of a democratic America, they were seen as profoundly patriotic, as the kind of critical questions that kept the American spirit alive—the kind of questions, incidentally, that our media were supposed to be pressing.

Can these schemes work? I don't think so. I think they are murderous, rapacious, and insane. But I don't know. Maybe they can. Similar schemes have worked in countries like Chile, where a democracy in which over 90 percent of the people voted has been reduced to one in which only about 20 percent vote because they say, as Americans are learning to say, that it no longer matters whom you vote for.

In the meantime, is there any hope, or do we just band together like lemmings and dive off a cliff? Yes, there is always hope, though at times it is more hidden, as it is now.

As some critics are now saying, and as I have been preaching and writing for almost twenty years, America's liberals need to grow beyond political liberalism, with its often self-absorbed focus on individual rights to the exclusion of individual responsibilities to the larger society. Liberals will have to construct a more complete vision with moral and religious grounding. That does not mean confessional Christianity. It means the legitimate heir to Christianity. Such a legitimate heir need not be a religion, though it must have clear moral power and be able to attract the minds and hearts of a voting majority of Americans.

And the new liberal vision must be larger than the conservative religious vision that will be appointing judges, writing laws, and bending the cultural norms toward hatred and exclusion for the foreseeable future. The conservatives deserve a lot of admiration. They have spent the last forty years studying American politics, forming their vision, and learning how to gain control of the political system. And it worked; they have won. Even if liberals can develop a bigger vision, they still have all that time-consuming work to do. It won't be quick. It isn't even clear that liberals will be willing to do it; they may instead prefer to go down with the ship they're used to.

One man who has been tireless in his investigations and critiques of America's slide into fascism is Michael C. Ruppert, whose postings usually read as though he is wound way too tight. But he offers four pieces of advice about what we can do now, and they seem reality-based enough to pass on to you. This is America; they're all about money:

- First, he says, you should get out of debt.
- Second is to spend your money and time on things that give you energy and provide you with useful information.
- Third is to stop spending a penny with major banks, news media, and corporations that feed you lies and leave you angry and exhausted.
- And fourth is to learn how money works and use it like a political weapon—as he predicts the rest of the world will be doing against us.

That's advice written recently. Another bit of advice comes from sixty years ago, from Roosevelt's vice president, Henry Wallace. He said, "Democracy, to crush fascism internally, must . . . develop the ability to keep people fully employed and at the same time balance the budget. It must put human beings first and dollars second. It must appeal to reason and decency and not to violence and deceit. We must not tolerate oppressive government or industrial oligarchy in the form of monopolies and cartels."

Still another way to understand fascism is as a kind of colonization. A simple definition of "colonization" is that it takes people's stories away and assigns them supportive roles in stories that empower others at their expense. When you are taxed to support a government that uses you as a means to serve the ends of others, you are—ironically—in a state of taxation without representation. That's where this country started, and it's where we are now.

I don't know the next step. I'm not a political activist; I'm only a preacher. But whatever you do, whatever we do, I hope that we can remember some very basic things that I think of as eternally true. One is that the vast majority of people are good and decent people who mean and do as well as they know how. Very few people are evil, though some are. But we all live in families where some of our blood relatives support things we hate. I believe they mean well, and the way to rebuild broken bridges is through greater understanding, compassion, and a reality-based story that is more inclusive and empowering for the vast majority of us.

Those who want to live in a reality-based story rather than as serfs in an ideology designed to transfer power, possibility, and hope to a small ruling elite have much long and hard work to do, individually and collectively. It will not be either easy or quick.

But we shall do it. We shall go forward in hope and in courage. Let us seek that better path and find the courage to take it—step, by step, by step.

PART THREE

AMERICA

9

Responding to the Violence of September 11

Septermber 16, 2001

Where do we begin? For me, it began in anger—in fury. When I heard of the destruction of the World Trade Center towers and a section of the Pentagon on Tuesday, I wanted bloody revenge. I thought, "Kill the bastards!" I didn't know just who the bastards were, but I wanted them dead.

Now, five days later, I see that angry theme is on the verge of becoming our country's battle cry, as we are being cranked up for a long and costly war against an invisible enemy—an enemy defined not by a country but by an ideology.

I can sympathize with the anger because I felt it too. These mass murders were reprehensible by any moral code. Civilized Christians, Jews, Muslims, Buddhists, Hindus, and all the rest condemn these actions as contemptible and against all of our highest values.

It is hard to know what to do, though it is suddenly very clear what we shall not do:

- We shall not react as Mother Teresa did when officials from Union Carbide flew her—after making a donation to her charities—to Bhopal, India, following the deaths of 2,000 people from Union Carbide's escaped chemicals. Met at the airport by the media, Mother Teresa was asked what message she brought to the suffering people, and she replied, "Just forgive, forgive." To forgive in these extreme cases is to condone, and we shall not condone these murders.

• Nor shall we follow the Christian teaching of "turn the other cheek." I haven't heard any ministers suggesting this and can't imagine it.

• We might follow the even older teaching of "an eye for an eye, a tooth for a tooth," a body for a body, carnage for carnage. I hope not, but our leaders and media pundits are trying to herd us in that direction, and they may succeed.

The wisest teaching I know of that still applies to these murders comes from Confucius when he said, 2,500 years ago, that we should repay good with kindness, but repay evil with justice. That seems the noblest and most humane goal here. We should strive to repay these deeds not with vengeance, but with justice.

But what is justice here? Justice might be defined as truth plus compassion plus power, or as love at a distance. And while it does not require that we love our enemy—a teaching for calmer situations that would be vulgar here—the quest for justice does require that we try to understand these people who threw away their lives, and nearly 3,000 American lives with them.

But to try and understand requires that we back off, and it may feel too soon to back off from the raw feelings of anger here. So please forgive me if it seems that I am backing off too far and too soon from an attack without precedent in our country's history.

The hardest part of trying to understand these attackers is in understanding that they didn't see this attack the way we do, just as they don't see us as we do.

The first thing we must understand is that this was *not* an attack on freedom or on democracy! The attackers made it crystal clear through their choice of targets what they were attacking. This was an attack arising from a deep hatred of our country's military and economic actions and policies, which they see as selfish, bloody, and evil.

To us, the Pentagon is the symbol of America's military strength, which we like to believe is used in the service of freedom, honor, and decency the world over. But there are many people in the world who don't see it that way. To them, the Pentagon is the symbol of a military might that serves a predatory nation.

We point to our 3,000 freshly dead brothers and sisters and say, "This is barbaric. How could you have done it?" We're right: it was barbaric, and no decent person should have done it. But they point to other lists of U.S. military actions that they also believe to be the work of terrorists.

They point to Iraq and the nearly complete sham of the Gulf War. We destroyed the water purification facilities ten years ago, and since then have carefully controlled through rationing and embargo how much chlorine and other chemicals needed to control water-borne diseases are permitted into Iraq. As a result of these continuing actions, an estimated one million Iraqis have died during that time, including over 500,000 children. "Where," they ask, "are your tears for these men, women, and children you have killed?"

They point to our invasion of Panama—an invasion made in violation of all international law. They remind us that we shelled a poor ghetto area of Panama City for several hours, shouting instructions to surrender over the bullhorn—in English, not Spanish—and then bulldozed the bodies of about 4,000 people, mostly civilians, into an unmarked mass grave. "Decent people cry for all the world's innocents. Where were your tears for these?" they wonder. What would we have felt if this had happened in one of our cities?

They point to our continued uncritical support for Israel,

again in opposition to the consensus of world opinion. Most
nations, they point out, agree that Israel's occupation of the West
Bank and Gaza is illegal and that there should be a Palestinian
state. It looks to many people in the world like we only appeal
to international law and a consensus of the world's people when
it suits our own selfish purposes. When it doesn't, we break the
laws like drunken, gun-toting bullies. We send $3 billion a year
in military aid to Israel: the guns and bombs that are killing their
Muslim or Arab relatives were made in the USA. "What about
your complicity in these acts of murder and terror?" they ask.

The list of military meddling could be extended by adding
more countries from South America and Africa, not to mention
Bosnia, Guatemala, Vietnam, and more. But these are a few of the
reasons that many people in the world hate us and believe our
military power is a symbol of selfishness and of evil.

The bigger targets and the bigger symbol, though, were
the twin towers of the World Trade Center in New York. This
attack wasn't about freedom or democracy or religion. It was
about economics. And these murdering fanatics represent a large
number of people who are neither murderers nor fanatics, who
see our country's economic behaviors and policies as greedy and
destructive to other nations.

None of this is new. People from all over the world have been
picketing and protesting the World Trade Organization and the
World Bank for years—though such protests don't get much
space or time in our media.

But these people see us as a country whose economic plan
includes managing and controlling the economies of other
nations.

We learned a few years ago that the Nike company had paid
Michael Jordan a promotional fee of $25 million, more than twice
the combined annual wages of all Asian workers in all companies

making our tennis shoes. Many people around the world wonder why that didn't bother us, why we didn't see it as a clear example of America's double standard.

They wonder why we don't see the same plan working in our own country. Our workers make less in real dollars than they did thirty years ago, while Bill Gates's personal fortune exceeds that of the bottom 40 percent of Americans combined. Our workers have fewer benefits, fewer unions, and less job security than they have had in decades. In the meantime, the pay of top executives has skyrocketed. This, say our critics, is the plan of America's economy, and our armies serve the interests of our wealthy elites.

These are among the reasons why the twin towers of the World Trade Center are seen as symbols of greed and evil, and why citizens and children in Egypt and elsewhere could be seen cheering their fall. Not because they are barbarians who hate our freedom, but because they are workers who hate our destructive economic plan and the military meddling that is its servant.

These people know full well that they can't match our military power. But they also know they don't have to. They learned, from watching us in Vietnam, that we do not know how to fight against guerrillas or terrorists, that we have no defense against individuals serving a powerful ideology who are willing to sacrifice their lives by becoming suicide bombers.

So what should we do? How should we respond? Several options are already presenting themselves.

We could just "bomb Afghanistan back into the Stone Age," as some have suggested, and as our president seems eager to do. The problem with bombing Afghanistan back to the Stone Age is that the Russians already did it a few years ago. Afghanistan is a desolate country with no real economy, few schools or hospitals, no infrastructure, and a population of hungry, powerless, and desperate people.

One Afghan has circulated an e-mail essay I read recently. I don't know if it is all correct, but I suspect it is close. He said the way to think correctly of the situation there is to see Osama bin Laden as a Hitler, the Taliban as the Nazis, and the Afghan people as the Jews in the prison camps. The Afghans aren't our enemies. They were just earlier victims of the others. Still, our leaders, aided by the rabble-rousing abilities of the media, seem poised to bomb Afghanistan until even the struggling life it has left is gone.

Another tactic that we're hearing is that of turning this into a battle of Caucasians against Arabs, and Christians against Muslims. This is a tactic that has worked well in our "war on drugs" by making white people fear black crack addicts—though most drug profits are made by white people. It is a "misdirection" tactic to divert us from the more vital events and schemes, but it too is gaining strength.

And a third tactic—likely to be used in combination with the first two—is a long and costly large-scale military campaign. This too seems to be in the works. Perhaps it will all come to pass.

But I want to back off from these imminent war plans and look at them quite differently than we are being trained to see them. I want to assume, with our critics, that this is primarily about economics, not anything of nobler virtue. And the fact that this is driven by corporations' concern for profits has dramatic and terrifying implications for the coming wars.

When—or, perhaps, if—we begin the massive, years-long War to End All Evil, it will be the greatest boon to the economic plan to convert us into a two-tiered economy of a powerful few ruling over the desperate many:

- Individual rights and democratic freedoms will be restricted for reasons of "national security." A culture of obedience will be established without effort, in a top-down hierarchical form that is the dream of every fascist.

- Religion will be subsumed under nationalism, and repressive religions will have the government's sanction. The Jerry Falwell and Pat Robertson clones will become our own version of the Taliban—weaker, but still frightening.

- The hundreds of billions of dollars needed for the war efforts will swallow all surpluses from our economy for years to come, leaving less for education, health insurance, unemployment, or any of the other government expenditures that give the lower classes a glimmer of hope or a step up.

This scenario is as cynical as it is ingenious (or at least fortuitous) for those working to complete the structural changes in our economy. If history and the nature of greed and power are any indications, it is what lies ahead for us.

There is another option. It wouldn't cost much, it could empower not only our people but nearly all people of the world, and it seems possible. At least, it is already being done. It's a lesson we can learn from the Irish.

Ireland has dealt with terrorism as a fact of life for decades. But in 1998, the vision and will of the people suddenly changed, and it has made all the difference. That was the year of the Omagh bombing, when a car bomb exploded in a crowded market, killing dozens of innocent shoppers. During the following week, as memorial services took place all over the island, a lot of people began saying "Enough!" Enough terrorism, enough violence. Some of the more psychopathic terrorists on both sides tried frightening the Irish back into the deadly status quo, but—so far, at least—they have not succeeded.

The Irish were not just saying "enough" to the violence perpetrated against them. They were saying enough to *all* violence. Terrorism and violence were no longer methods they would tolerate or accept. It has been just three years, but so far it is still working there.

Could the American people be awakened and stirred enough to say enough? It couldn't mean just "enough violence from Muslim terrorists." It would also have to mean "enough violence from the U.S. government." It would be a public refusal to allow the kind of arrogant militarism in the service of economic greed that has marked us for decades. It would mean refusing to be the good Germans who know, but ignore, their own country's violence against others.

Such a move, a move with the courage the Irish are now showing, could empower the majority of people throughout the world and raise Americans to a role of leadership future generations would remember and adore. Christian, Muslim, Jewish, Hindu, Buddhist, you name it—the vast majority of people on earth hate this violence and are disgusted by terrorist activities from all directions.

If we began, if we found that vision compelling enough to be converted to an insistence on peaceful and respectful means, we could have the power to short-circuit our government's greedy and bloody plans—plans that will be written in our blood, not theirs, after all. We could change the face and the course of history, and avoid the bloody and insane chapter that is now beginning.

There is a Buddhist story with some wisdom to offer here, one from the Samurai tradition. The Samurai warriors were known for two things: skill with a sword and a high, uncompromising moral code. This Samurai warrior had tracked down an evil man whose deeds called for death. Finally cornering his foe, the warrior closed in to kill him. Suddenly, the man stepped forward and spat in the Samurai's face. The warrior flushed, sheathed his sword, and left. His culture called for him to kill for only the highest reasons. When the man spat in his face, he realized that if he were to kill him now, it would be out of personal rage, not noble ideals.

Please understand, I'm not suggesting that what happened to us this past Tuesday was in any way like merely having someone spit in our face! It was not. It was a bloody, cowardly, vile mass murder. But it has moved us to the point where we can be whipped up by our leaders and the media into murdering many others out of our rage, rather than from any higher or nobler motives.

If we do that, we shall not only demean ourselves and our nation, but we shall also flood the earth with rivers of blood—almost all of it from innocent people. It is fine to wave the American flag—I'm proud of this country too, when it lives up to its highest callings. But to wave the flag over vengeance from low motives is not to honor our history, but to dishonor it.

And so it seems a way out is offered, at least if we are truly people of noble character. Will we take it? Will we find the collective courage and resolve to say, and mean, enough? I don't know. I am only a preacher, not a prophet. All I have right now are prayers, and this is my prayer.

The Aftermath of 9/11

SEPTEMBER 23, 2001

Every generation, it seems, has its defining moment, the watershed event when we suddenly realize that the world isn't as we thought, we're not as safe as we thought, perhaps not as innocent as we thought. In that moment, a new generation is rudely and painfully taken forever out of a world of innocence and naïve trust.

There aren't many of these moments. They stand out in history as dates we'll never forget:

- December 7, 1941, "the day that lived in infamy," was such a moment, and the world never again felt quite as safe to those who lived through it.
- November 22, 1963, was unforgettable for people who grew up when I did. We all remember where we were and what we were doing when we heard that President John F. Kennedy had been murdered in Dallas. The world never seemed quiet as innocent or safe again.
- December 8, 1980, took me by surprise when I was in graduate school and I was stunned to see how powerfully it affected people in their twenties—it was the day that John Lennon was murdered. And I remember how many of them cried, held each other, and talked about not feeling safe anymore.

And now September 11, 2001, has joined the list of indelible moments. For many people it was the first time that the world didn't feel safe. There's a loss of innocence and a loss of naïve trust in the world that happens at these powerful moments, and it shatters the feeling that life is completely trustworthy and sacred and nourishing.

That's something we all went through twelve days ago. What comes next is something that many here have not been through and something that many others here have been through and that's the threat, the noise, and probably the reality of war. As one who's been through a war, all the feelings coming over the airwaves and coming from speeches of leaders are suddenly very familiar. I feel like I know what we're getting into and what's next.

When people are threatened, they band together within a common identity, and war offers one of the oldest and deepest and most powerful senses of reconnection that we can find. You can unite a country of 280 million people with a war against a common enemy, even an invisible enemy without a country, without a religion, without boundaries—it is enough to unite us as one people, with one voice, one God, and one purpose. It is seductive as hell. War makes everything simple, and it comes at a time when the complexity of things overwhelms us all.

War gives us very stark, black-and-white pictures of everything: a war for infinite justice, to end all evil, in a world so simple that all countries are either for us or against us. Never mind the fact that British and other European newspapers for years have been writing that our country has created the economic and military conditions that foster the hatred. Never mind that in other parts of the world this story has been written only in nuances and grays. Here it is black and white. It's cowboy logic—you are either for us or against us. It is simpleminded and seductive.

I thought of this when I began watching the interviews on television. The news is managed and selected for the effect it will have on the viewing audience. And the effect that's desired on the viewing audience is that it should unite us, with one voice and one God behind one goal, without quarrelsome questions.

I saw the interview with the wife of that brave man on the fourth plane who was part of a crew that fought with the hijackers and succeeded in crashing the plane into the ground killing all aboard rather than letting them fly the plane into another building—perhaps the Capitol, perhaps the White House. The man was an unqualified hero—as were his compatriots.

But there were lots of relatives and friends of heroes who wouldn't have said that what got them through it was their faith in God and the knowledge that their loved ones were in heaven where they would see them again. The interview with that woman provided the combination of the right religious message, the right image, and the right words to support the speeches that had just been heard in the Capitol that were chosen to be aired.

Every bit of news we see is going to have been chosen for us and carefully selected. The other way of saying this is that there are nuances and there are stories and facts and details that will not be printed and will not be aired and that we may not find out about for a year, if ever.

I don't know what they'll be in this new war, but I do know what some of the carefully avoided facts and stories were in our last war. So I'll take the Gulf War of 1991 as an example. You could also go back to the Vietnam War and mention the Pentagon Papers, which brought about a tremendous amount of disillusionment in people who discovered how intricate the scheming had been to deceive the American people. But from the Gulf War there are two stories I'll tell you. And I wonder if you have heard either of them. If you have not, you need to be very worried.

The first appeared in a one-paragraph story in the inside of the December 3, 1990, issue of *Newsweek*, about six weeks before the Gulf War was declared on January 15, 1991. After several months of all of us being told that the reason that we had to send troops to Kuwait was because hundreds of thousands of Iraqi troops had crossed over the border into Kuwait and it was a desperate situation that demanded a strong and large military force, the *Newsweek* item appeared under the headline "Where Are the Troops?"

The item said that some independent investigators had bought satellite photos and had hired retired CIA people to interpret them. They were recent satellite photos taken of the Iraq-Kuwait border area during the time that Iraqi troops were said to have passed on the highway into Kuwait. One photograph from mid-August showed the empty highway leading from Iraq to Kuwait. At one point a large sand dune had blown over about two-thirds of the highway, making it barely passable. A second photograph from mid-November showed the same highway, and by now the sand dune had blown all the way across the highway. It was covered completely between August and November. No troops had been driven down that highway.

The satellite photo was so precise that it showed the make of the aircraft, showed no troop formation or locations anywhere in Kuwait. We think that about 2,000 members of the Republican Guard of the elite Iraqi troops were in Kuwait, and that's a large force. But it's not 200,000 or 300,000. Where were the troops? Those photographs were published on the front page of the St. Petersburg, Florida, paper on January 6, 1991. Once war was declared nine days later, to the best of my knowledge, they were not published in any newspaper in the United States for the rest of 1991. At the end of 1991, the *Columbia Journalism Review*, which does this sort of thing every year as a watchdog, listed that story as one of the ten most underreported stories of 1991. Can you say "understatement"?

The second story concerns what happened shortly before the vote was taken to declare war on Iraq and to send American troops into Kuwait. The U.S. Senate voted for war by a majority of only five votes. The vote came not long after some terribly poignant testimony by a young, fifteen-year-old girl named Nayirah. She testified that she had been in the hospital nurseries in Kuwait when Iraqi soldiers came in and bayoneted babies, took them out of their incubators, and threw them on the floor. It was a repulsive, gut-wrenching story. After the vote, at least six of our congressmen said publicly that they were going to vote against the war until they heard Nayirah's testimony and changed their minds to vote in favor of the war.

But the story that Nayirah told was a complete fiction. She was the daughter of Kuwait's ambassador to the United States. The Kuwaitis had hired Hill & Knowlton, one of the largest public relations firms in America, to help them prepare a story that would convince America to send our soldiers to protect their—and our—oil interests. The story was concocted by Hill & Knowlton and rehearsed with Nayirah, who had not been anywhere near Kuwait at the time.

Now if you didn't know this, at least know that this story is a measure of how completely and how effectively we can be deceived and misled during the atmosphere of war, because it will certainly happen again. I don't know what facts or stories will be invented or buried this time, but it will happen again.

The same thing happens in religion that happens in politics. The theology of war is a very different theology from the theology of peace in any religion. The theology of peace—whether it's Christian, Muslim, or any other—is a theology with a very big God but no army. In a theology of peace we sing hymns and read poems about how we are all brothers and sisters, how there are no significant distinctions between races, nations, sexes, or anything else—we are all children of the same God. It's a very big God.

The theology of war is the reverse. Churches are expected to, and do, provide a theology for war—or theology for imperialism, if you like. And now it's a very small God and a very big army. If you want to read the theology of war, there are two places you can read it right now. It's the same theology in two different religions. You can see it clearly in statements from the Taliban and in statements from the likes of Christian fundamentalists such as Jerry Falwell and Pat Robertson—their hatred for the sexual aspects of American culture, especially liberated women, abortion, and homosexuality.

It's a list of a very tiny in-group and a very large out-group, and it's focused to be able to direct anger and hatred and weaponry against the source of evil. This reminds me of a Native American story that I just heard this week.

A young boy went to see his grandfather because he was angry that one of his friends had committed a terrible injustice against him and he wanted revenge, and he wanted his grandfather's advice on how to get revenge. His grandfather sat him down and said, "I know these feelings. I've had them myself. I too have had the feelings of hatred and anger and lust for blood and a lust for revenge. It's as though there were two wolves inside of me fighting to control my soul. One is a good wolf who takes care of its pups and who is a peaceful wolf that only fights when it's necessary and only as far as it's necessary. And the other wolf is an angry, angry, angry wolf that strikes out in all directions whenever it's given a chance.

"And these two wolves," the grandfather added, "are inside of me all the time fighting to dominate my soul." The grandson thought about it for a second and he said, "I don't get it grandfather, which wolf wins?"

And the grandfather said, "The one that I feed."

We have those two wolves now fighting for control of our soul as a nation and fighting for control of our individual souls. And the wolf that wins will be the wolf that we feed. I can't resolve this problem here. But we need to say it out loud. We're in a time of great pain and hurting. More than 3,000 people have been killed. We have no idea how many people on what will now be called "the other side" will be killed. We may wonder what to do about our hurt and about our deep sense of disconnection.

There's another story for us here, about a woman who was sad to the core of her soul because she had lost her son. She went to see a wise man and she said, "I'm hurting so much I cannot go on with life because of the sorrow I feel for the loss of my son. There must be some magic potion or spell or something you can do to make all the hurt go away." The wise man said, "You're very lucky that you came to me. There is such a magic to make the hurt and the sorrow go away. All you have to do is bring me a mustard seed, a tiny mustard seed, from the home of someone who has never known sorrow."

So the woman went around, first to the palaces, because certainly, she thought, rich people don't know any sorrow. And she heard at every palace and every castle story after story of people who had lost a daughter, lost a son, people who had been visited by horrible tragedies, by diseases, by all of the woes of humankind. And each time she heard one of these stories from one of these families, she'd stop and stay with them for a while to help them, because she knew what it was like to feel sorrow and she knew how to help them.

And after several such visits to families and people who had known sorrow and stopping to help them, the woman finally realized that the sage she consulted had been right. That magical mustard seed was the seed within her that made her reach out her own hand to take the hand of others who suffered.

In our days and weeks and months ahead, I hope that we can find ways to reach out our hands to help those others who are suffering, here and abroad.

II

Under the Cover of War

APRIL 21, 2002

How do you command and control others to get them to serve your agenda rather than their own? How do you colonize people?

This sounds like a political coup, so we think of things like armies, guns, loud noises, and the smell of gunpowder. But these loud and rude acts only give you the opportunity to win people's minds and hearts. Really to win them, or to colonize them, takes more subtle means. Still, it can be put simply: To control people, you need to write their story. You need to write the rules of the game that assign them supporting roles in a story that benefits you—and get them to want to do this.

Most religious teaching teaches us that we live in stories. These are our life stories, our myths, and our necessary fictions. On a personal level, there are many such stories: be pure, be reliable, be hard-working, be witty and popular, prove that Daddy was right about us, or prove that Daddy wasn't right about us. We have, between us, hundreds of such personal life scripts that assign us some of our life roles.

But I want to talk about larger stories today. I want to back off and look at the stories we live out, and live out of, as a society. This too could get complex, but I want to keep it simple, by looking at our "official" story—that we are a democracy—and the real story that has usually controlled our society: that we are some kind of an aristocracy. Democracy, while a high and noble-sounding ideal, is such an unlikely form of government!

Since the seventeenth century, there have been two primary stories that have vied with each other for control of American society.

In the language of those writers, it was the choice between rule by the "masters of mankind" and "the majority of mankind." It is the rule of the many by the few, or of all by the many. It is the choice between an aristocracy and a democracy.

Which is better? We have all been trained to answer, "Democracy, of course!" But opinions have always been divided on this, as they are today, and even in this room. John Locke, the English philosopher who influenced many of our own Founding Fathers, thought it must be an aristocracy because he didn't trust the masses. He said that "day-laborers and tradesmen, the spinsters and dairymaids" must be told what to believe. "The greatest part cannot know and therefore they must believe," he said. Many still agree with him.

Thomas Jefferson took the other side. He said aristocrats are "those who fear and distrust the people, and wish to draw all powers from them into the hands of the higher classes." Jefferson's "democrats," on the other hand, "identify with the people, have confidence in them, cherish and consider them as honest and safe. . . ."

The one story seeks government through command and control; the other, through empowerment and trust. You can already hear which one is more vulnerable and less likely to win, can't you?

Still, there's a tactical problem. How will the more powerful and wealthy, for example, pull this off, when they are the distinct minority? For all our history, this battle between aristocrats and democrats has continued. For the first 150 years of our nation's history, it sometimes seemed like a continuous battle between those who had money and power, and everybody else. The courts (sometimes) kept regulating the aristocrats through laws and statutes that limited their ability to earn profits at the expense of the rest of the country.

The country, when it had a choice, wasn't buying the story the aristocrats were trying to sell, and people weren't willing to spend their lives as servants of the few. Here is the long story of labor disputes, monopoly, antitrust laws, and other rulings designed to protect the rights of the majority from the extra power and skill of those who would be their rulers. If you know much American history, you already know all this. There's nothing new here.

But in the twentieth century, something new came along: mass communication, along with its dark child, propaganda. Propaganda became an obsession of American leaders after World War One. "Propaganda has only one object," wrote one of its early masters, "to conquer the masses." Propaganda is the tool used by a small minority to sell their story to a large majority. With enough slick spin, emotional power, and appeal to elemental yearnings and powerful symbols (as in "God bless America"), a few brilliant visionaries can convert and control an entire nation.

After World War One, people on both sides of the Atlantic wrote about this new invention. Adolph Hitler praised the British and said the main reason that Germany lost the war was because its propaganda was so inferior to the British. He vowed to learn from the British. And in this country too, President Woodrow Wilson formed a new group to adapt techniques of using propaganda to influence the American people in desired directions. This was in the 1920s.

The great American journalist Walter Lippmann was in President Wilson's propaganda organization, along with Edward Bernays, who could be called the father of American propaganda. Bernays led the transfer of wartime propaganda skills to business's peacetime problems of coping with democracy. When the war ended, he wrote, business "realized that the great public could now be harnessed to their cause as it had been harnessed during the war to the national cause, and the same methods could do the job."

And the payoff? In the words of one of these early propagandists: "If the others let a minority conquer the state, then they must also accept the fact that we will establish a dictatorship." And so ends democracy. Once a group learns how to manipulate the masses to its own ends, democracy dies, replaced by a dictatorship, a rule of the few, an aristocracy. This last quote came from Joseph Goebbels, Hitler's minister of propaganda. It was also Goebbels who said that propaganda's one object was to conquer the masses, just as he described the masses as "the weak, cowardly, lazy majority of people."

But the masses—and you realize, I hope, that this means us—weren't thought of any more highly on this side of the Atlantic. Walter Lippmann wrote of the "ignorance and stupidity of the masses." The general public, he said, were mere "ignorant and meddlesome outsiders," who must not intrude in the management of public affairs, though they may be permitted to select periodically among the "responsible men" whose task it is to rule them.

Do you see that this is the tool the aristocracy had needed since our country began? The invention of propaganda and its immediate use after World War One is one of the most important stories of the twentieth century.

Propaganda was talked about pretty openly during its early years—before the people who were practicing it realized that wasn't a very smart thing to do. In 1934, the new president of the American Political Science Association said in his presidential address that government should be in the hands of "an aristocracy of intellect and power," not directed by "the ignorant, the uninformed."

"The public must be put in its place," added Walter Lippmann, so that the "responsible men" may "live free of the trampling and the roar of a bewildered herd" as they rule them. That "bewildered herd"—that would be us.

This is a chapter of American history we must know if we are to understand who is running our country and how they are running it. But we don't know it, do we? Why do you suppose that is?

Alex Carey wrote in *Taking the Risk Out of Democracy* that there were three key developments in the twentieth century that have shaped the world we're living in today: the growth of democracy, the growth of corporate power, and the growth of corporate propaganda as a means of protecting corporate power against democracy.

Corporate propaganda directed toward the public has two main goals: to identify the free-enterprise system in popular consciousness with every cherished value and to identify interventionist governments and strong unions—the only forces capable of checking the complete domination of society by corporations—with tyranny, oppression, and subversion. The techniques used to do this are variously called "public relations," "corporate communications," and "economic education."

Corporate propaganda directed inward to employees has the purpose of weakening the links between employees and their unions. From about 1920 through the present, U.S. business made great progress toward the ideal of a democracy managed through corporate propaganda. Those who were entrusted with corporate power realized that one of the best investments they can make is to buy the politicians who make the laws.

Current struggles to pass meaningful campaign finance reform are attempts to rein in the power of corporations. But for the past couple of decades, many or most of our major political candidates have become, like used BMWs, "preowned vehicles." To get the money they need to compete in American elections, they must get large investments from large business interests. And for those investments, they owe their investors the effort to slant the laws of the land in ways that let the investors feed at the public trough.

What does this mean? It means weakening or eliminating controls on environmental pollution or toxic emissions or burial of radioactive waste, letting chemical companies like Monsanto infect the entire continent's wheat and corn crops with genetically modified organisms that have not been, and cannot be, tested. It means reducing the taxes corporations pay and shifting that tax burden to the citizens. It means breaking unions and redefining the economy as one that revolves around the price of stocks rather than the ability of regular citizens to earn good livings through an honest day's work.

You can see how the paybacks from investing in elections work by looking at Texas's own, Enron's former CEO Kenneth Lay, the biggest single investor in George W. Bush's campaign for president. In return for this investment, Lay was able to name government regulators, shape energy policies, and block the regulation of offshore tax havens. Moreover, Enron had "intimate contact with Taliban officials," and the energy giant's much-reviled Dabhol project in India was set to benefit from a hookup with the oil pipeline we planned to run through Afghanistan.

These negotiations collapsed in August 2001—a date that should make our ears prick up—when the Taliban asked the United States to help reconstruct Afghanistan's infrastructure and provide a portion of the oil supply for local needs. The U.S. response was reportedly succinct: "We will either carpet you in gold or carpet you in bombs." Was the Taliban really destroyed for harboring terrorists? Or was it destroyed for failing to further the ambitions of Texas millionaires?

The London newspaper the *Guardian* also reports that U.S. State Department officials in early July 2001 informed their Russian and Pakistani counterparts of possible plans to invade Afghanistan in the fall. Once we began our new war, it provided a cover for other agendas that the Bush administration had been trying to move on since the election to fulfill promises to their corporate investors.

I read in early March that over $212 billion was transferred from our economy to our larger corporations in the form of retroactive tax refunds, some refunds dating back fifteen years. Huge tax refunds were voted in, from which well over 90 percent went to the richest 1 percent of Americans. These are some of the returns on their investments in the president's campaign.

News reports from *Der Spiegel* to the London *Observer*, from the *Los Angeles Times* to MSNBC to CNN, all indicate that many different warnings were received by the administration before the 9/11 attacks. It has even been reported that the U.S. government broke bin Laden's secure communications before September 11. The U.S. government is being sued today by survivors of the embassy bombings because, from court reports, it appears clear that the United States had received prior warnings then too, but did nothing to protect the staffs at our embassies. Did the same thing happen again?

I read an article in the March/April issue of the *Humanist* magazine that's worth sharing. In the days leading up to 9/11, thousands of "put" options were purchased on companies whose stocks tanked after September 11. Put options are bought by investors when they are willing to gamble that a company's stock price will go down in the near future. Most prominent among these companies are American Airlines and United Airlines, whose planes hit the Twin Towers, and the investment firms of Morgan Stanley and Merrill Lynch, whose offices were destroyed in the towers.

On September 6 and 7, investors purchased 4,744 put options in United Airlines at the Chicago Board Options Exchange. At the same time, only 396 "call" options—where an investor bets on a stock price increasing—were purchased. On September 10, investors bought 4,516 put options in American Airlines versus 748 call options. In the three days prior to September 11, investors bought 2,157 put options in Morgan Stanley, a company that occupied twenty floors of offices at the World Trade Center. Volume during the previous week was a mere 27 put options per day. Likewise, investors bought another 12,215 put options for World Trade Center tenant Merrill Lynch.

Most embarrassing to the government, however, is the fact that many of the mysterious put options were purchased through an investment firm that was formally headed by Buzzy Krongard, the current executive director of the CIA.

Under the cover of war, I believe there is a good chance that we are losing our American way of life, our civil freedoms, our economy, and the remaining vestiges of our democracy. Where does this leave us? It reconnects me with some of my strongest and most basic convictions:

- We cannot lose faith. We must continue to appeal to the better angels of our nature, and the better angels of our leaders.
- We cannot lose hope. The future is not yet written, its options are still open.
- We must try not to become self-righteous or mean-spirited, or attempt to harm our nation. We may and must criticize and chastise its errant ways. But we must struggle to do it in a spirit of love. I struggle mightily with this one, and often lose here.

I hope and I pray that we may indeed add our critical and caring voices to the dialogue. And even though we are few and our efforts may seem meager, they are essential—for us, for our nation, and for the world.

PART FOUR

HONEST RELIGION

The Legitimate Heir to God

The Buddhists tell a wonderful story that sounds simple, even funny, like a child's tale. But it's one of the most revolutionary stories ever told.

A man was on one side of a river that was dangerous and treacherous while on the other side was safety. So he used logs, branches, leaves, grass, and twigs and built a raft and, using his hands and feet, propelled himself to safety on the other side. Once across the river, he was so grateful that he put the raft on his back and decided to carry it everywhere for the rest of his life.

The Buddha told this parable and asked the monks whether this was a good idea. They did not think so. The Buddha agreed and said the raft worked once, but now the man must put it down and go on his way, because his next passage may not need a raft at all, but a vehicle of a very different kind.

We must be prepared to change vehicles—including our beliefs about ourselves, about relationships, about work, about our nation, or about God—if we are going to use beliefs wisely rather than foolishly. For beliefs are only useful if they help us through the transitions we are facing, not if we are carrying them on our backs, or sticking with them because they were prescribed by someone authoritative.

This is really one of the most empowering stories ever written because it encourages heresy, it sanctions experimentation, and it endorses change. It trusts us more than our religions, trusts us to know what kind of a vehicle we might need at any point, trusts us to change vehicles—and grants us the authority to do so. When you apply this to religion, it could get you burned at the stake in most times and places. But it's profound and wise. Sometimes even our religions become like rafts that must be put down as we search for their legitimate heir, one that can carry us through tough transitions with integrity and hope.

For instance, the more our current administration in Washington claims it's being guided by God, the more warlike, greedy, and imperialistic it seems to become. If you take these officials at their word, they are Christians—or at least people who believe in God, since they mention God a lot more than they mention Jesus. And if that is how the word "God" is being defined and used in our society, then we need a different way of talking about what Abraham Lincoln called the "better angels of our nature." We need a legitimate heir to it, and fast!

On the surface, this just sounds rude. While America was never founded as a Christian nation, Christianity has still been the dominant religion here since we began. So whether we are Christians or not, our whole society is shot through with the symbols and myths of Christianity. The song "Blowin' in the Wind" that we sang this morning was a protest song, and part of the message was that whatever was carrying our notions of decency, civility, and peaceful behavior—whatever the vehicles of our nobler aspirations were, they were failing. We needed a legitimate heir to the culture that said "yes" to an immoral war and "no" to decent treatment of even our own people.

History shows us that all gods die, though the great ones die more slowly, and can linger in a moribund state for centuries. They can die in several ways. They can die when the cosmology supporting them collapses. They can die when they no longer inspire passion or affection in people's hearts. And they can die when their stories and symbols are more easily hijacked by preachers and politicians of low and mean purpose than by those of high and noble purpose.

And all these things have happened during the past couple centuries to the primary God of our American culture.

But here's my question: Why does the God of Western religions need an heir, and what does it mean to be a "legitimate heir"?

One measure is political: the degree to which only the very lowest forms of Christianity have attracted the political and military power in our time. Pat Robertson has said that a democracy is a terrible form of government unless it is run by his kind of Christians—the kind that will not tax the rich, will not support social services, welfare, or public education, and so on. And the Reverend Jerry Falwell said during a television interview a couple of weeks ago that we should hunt down terrorists and blow them away in the name of the Lord.

Jesus would detest these men. Don't be shocked, that's not an overstatement. Heck, Jesus called Peter Satan, and that was just because Peter didn't understand him! Peter wasn't even offering to blow people away in the name of God. Jesus would detest these men and the low and hateful religion they sell.

The God of people like Robertson and Falwell—and a growing number of other bad preachers—is not a God worth serving and has nothing to do with the far higher teachings of a Jesus who instructed people to love one another and not to judge one another, and who said that whatever we did to the least among us we did to him. The God Jerry Falwell worships is little more than his own bigotries, writ large and nasty. And ironically, the fact that he can proudly chant such hateful and murderous advice while holding a Bible shows that he doesn't really believe in the God of Jesus for one second and knows that nothing will happen to him for insulting the very idea of God with his smallness.

That's the measure of a religion whose god has died. And when gods die, their corpses almost always become hand puppets for the worst kind of charlatans and demagogues. Conversely, and importantly, when a god can *become* the hand puppet of men like these, it is a sign that that god is dying.

This has happened before. When Franco (Francisco Franco Bahamonde, 1892–1975) established his fascist dictatorship in Spain, he brought the Catholic Church into power with him—though, again, just the low and mean parts that oppressed women, the poor, and the different. But when Franco's reign finally ended, so did the power of the church. People had seen that it became the willing toady of the worst kind of people all too eagerly, and they didn't trust it with their hearts or minds. In some ways, Spain now has a more liberal set of abortion laws than our own country does. That's a sign of the church losing authority in people's minds and hearts, and it happened because the religion seemed like far too natural a bedmate for fascism.

And now Spain's new president Zapatera is cutting the state subsidy of the Catholic Church and vowing to establish a completely secular government, with higher moral and ethical standards than the church brought them.

In our own country, the phrase "Christo-fascism" is beginning to appear in more and more places—Google it, and you'll find an increasing number of hits. Some feel it is happening here. I'm one of them. And once again, the religion seems more available as a tool for the rich, greedy, powerful, and mean than for the poor, for whom Jesus spoke. Jesus didn't think rich people could even get into heaven.

A second reason the raft won't float is scientific. It's that the symbols and myths of Christianity lost their footing in the real world more than two centuries ago, as the best Christian thinkers have pointed out for at least that long. Western religions were grounded in the idea of a male god who was a being. He walked, talked, saw, heard, planned, rewarded, and punished. To do these things, he had to live somewhere, and eventually they assigned him to heaven, which they believed was right above the sky.

But during the past couple of centuries, we have realized there is nothing above the sky but endless space. God lost a place to live. And that means—though few people want to talk about it—that we lost the kind of god who could do human-type things like seeing, hearing, or loving. We haven't finished this revolution yet, but it is a profound one.

If somebody tells you that God wants you to do something, you should be asking how you could check that out for yourself, independently. If there is not a way—and it's not clear how there could be a way—then the command doesn't come from a god. It's the command of those who have turned the corpse of this god into their hand puppet to serve their agenda—often at your expense.

Now, we could go on listing all the logical or scientific or commonsense reasons that the myths and symbols of Christianity have lost any deep roots in our modern consciousness, but it wouldn't achieve much. Because religions aren't primarily vehicles of truth about the world. Primarily, they are like the rafts in that Buddhist parable—rafts to carry us across certain kinds of human dilemmas, with honest insights into the human condition and wisdom to help us live wisely and well.

It's true that once we've been helped by a religion we tend to carry that raft around on our backs from then on, whether it's the right vehicle for us or not. But it's more true that we need some kind of a vehicle for our hopes, dreams, yearnings, and tender mercies. And the very best stories and teachings of Christianity honor those, even if its loudest and most powerful preachers and adherents do not.

So it isn't enough to set the raft down. A legitimate heir to God would have to carry our yearnings and help us live better lives.

Neither morality nor ethics rely on religion as their vehicles—and that's good news. Across Europe, for instance, religion has lost its power of persuasion. Only about 1 or 2 percent of the English and French attend church; it's only a few points higher in Germany. And as a nation, Japan is officially secular. Even closer to home, so is Canada, whose ties with Catholicism are little more than ornamental. Yet these cultures have moral standards at least as high as ours. For instance, they all have lower infant mortality rates and higher educational standards than we do. They all have far fewer citizens without basic health insurance than we do, and they all have higher standards of living for their citizens over age sixty-five than we do. And in Germany and the Netherlands, all citizens who want it are given a free college education, because the government believes that informed citizens able to think for themselves are preferable to ignorant citizens who just obey orders.

Don't think of these as merely "political" values. These are profoundly religious values. They show the souls of these nations. They show how these nations regard others, how they treat their own weakest members, and whether their "pro-life" stance is dishonest rhetoric. If the tree is known by its fruits, as Jesus said, then America is the least religious and compassionate country in the developed world!

So we look outward to a world of countries that are more moral and ethical than we are, though far less religious in the official sense. Some say this means that all religion is bad. I don't agree. I say it means that bad religion should be dropped like a hot raft. I want us, both individually and collectively, to develop a more adequate religion, and a more adequate sense of compassion and responsibility toward others than our national policies reflect.

It can happen within Christianity or any other religion—if that religion can be raised to its higher levels of aspiration rather than sinking to its lower ones. It can also be done without any organized religion.

But however it is done and wherever it is done, it needs to inspire us and needs to inspire our nation to change its direction from a greedy, selfish, imperialistic nation that is now disliked or detested by most other countries in the world.

Here are seven things I think the legitimate heir to God will have to have:

1. It must be reality based, consistent with the findings of our best contemporary sciences. Pretending the Grand Canyon is only 6,000 years old is an insult to the intelligence of an attentive twelve-year-old and not worthy of us. If you can't serve truth, you can't serve God. And ignorant ideology does not trump truth, except under fascism and its religious form, fundamentalism.

2. It must be inclusive and expansive. The Greeks pictured the completed human being as a series of concentric circles. In the center was just the individual, then the relationships that expanded the individual's awareness, compassion, and responsibility. Then came friends, other citizens, and society, then the world, all of history, and all the high ideals often associated with gods, but that the Greeks of 2,400 years ago associated with our own fuller humanity.

3. It must be compelling, even commanding. Conservative Christians speak of the need to feel "convicted" before we can see the light, and this is true. We must not only hear of higher possibilities, but also be awakened, "convicted," and converted by them.

4. It must be—in Origen's wonderful third-century phrase—both "useful to us, and worthy of God." And "God" means the highest set of demands we can articulate, the highest ideals, the most inclusive attitude, and the most demanding kind of life. The way, as Jesus and many others have said, is very narrow, and not many enter it.

5. It must be the biggest, most inclusive, most compassionate framework we can imagine—otherwise, it wouldn't be worthy of the name "God," let alone God's legitimate heir. And it must be both more accepting and more demanding of us than psychology, politics, religion, or nationalism can be. Why must it be bigger? Because in a pluralistic world where people hold many conflicting beliefs, you either need a larger God, or a larger army. The path of nationalism and imperialism is always to go for the army; the path of honest religion is to try and articulate a larger concept of God—by whatever name it's called forth.

6. It must give us life. That's the mark of a god. The basic covenant people make with their gods is always the same, and it's very simple. We say, "I'll serve you heart, mind, and body. I'll give my life into your service." Then whatever we have made into our god must give us a life worth living. If it can't do that, it isn't a real god, but a phony.

7. It must be a bigger vehicle than the raft our society is offering us under the banner of approved Christianity. We need a larger vehicle for the wisdom that has helped the great religions to endure in the hearts and minds of countless generations of people who are trying to grow into their full humanity, trying to grow into children of God, to realize their Buddha nature, to understand

that atman really is one with Brahman, to incarnate the rhythms and rules of the Tao, and to act out of that infinite and eternal identity rather than something lesser.

All these are saying about the same thing, in the jargon of their individual religions. In a pluralistic world, however, jargon just separates us. We need to be brought together, and that means we need to be able to say what we actually believe—in ordinary language—so people in other religions can understand us, and can realize that we're not so different after all. And the more we can put these things in ordinary language, the easier it will be to communicate with people of good character, no matter what their nationality or religion, because these are the goals of all decent religion. So this rebirth can happen within any existing religion.

Finding the next step, the legitimate heir to what was once called God, is one of the biggest and most important steps people can take. And it is taken, like so many things, one step at a time.

But spend some time with this, will you? Spend some time asking what you really believe, what beliefs you think might guide you better than the pronouncements about God you're hearing—and will be hearing more of from our worst leaders. We say we're all in this together. But first, we must all be in this search for beliefs worth living by. It's your move. It's our move. Like always.

13

Reclaiming Our Highest Ideals from Religion

JANUARY 2, 2005

Someone sent me an essay from the British paper the *Guardian* on Christmas Eve, written by an Anglican priest, the Reverend Dr. Giles Fraser of Oxford. He is making a distinction between the religion *of* Jesus and the religions *about* Jesus, and he does it so well I want to share some of it with you.

> Nicene Christianity is the religion of Christmas and Easter, the celebration of a Jesus who is either too young or too much in agony to shock us with his revolutionary rhetoric. The adult Christ who calls his followers to renounce wealth, power and violence is passed over in favour of the gurgling baby and the screaming victim. As such, Nicene Christianity is easily conscripted into a religion of convenience, with believers worshipping a gagged and glorified savior who has nothing to say about how we use our money or whether or not we go to war.
>
> . . . In a similar vein, modern evangelical choruses offer wave upon wave of praise to the name of Jesus, but offer little political or economic content to trouble his adoring fans. . . .
>
> . . . Like Constantine, George Bush has borrowed

the language of Christianity to support and justify his military ambition. And just like that of Constantine, the Christianity of this new Rome offers another carefully edited version of the Bible. Once again, the religion that speaks of forgiving enemies and turning the other cheek is pressed into military service.

Bush may have claimed that "Jesus Christ changed my life," but Jesus doesn't seem to have changed his politics.

This piece is saying that normative Christianity not only has nothing to do with the message of Jesus, but that it exists to *stifle* that message as its mortal *enemy*. And yet, Reverend Fraser isn't giving evangelical religion—which has nothing to do with Jesus—the credit it deserves. Not theological credit—there, he is dead on in noting that it is a stark betrayal of Jesus, the man. But political credit—for evangelical religion, put into the service of military power and economic greed, now has more power, at least in America, than it ever had before.

It reminds me of a story from the field of music, which I want to use as a lens through which to view the rise of literalistic Christianity—what is being called Christo-fascism—in America.

When he was a young man, the composer Claude Debussy earned money as a music critic. Once, he was reviewing a new opera by Richard Wagner, the acknowledged master of virtually every facet of music, drama, and staging. Most saw him as the dawn of a new era of music. But Debussy saw something else. "Wagner," he wrote, "is the sunset which some have mistaken for a sunrise." Even with all the attention Wagner was getting, Debussy saw him as the end of an era. And history proved Debussy right.

It has been observed for decades that in some respects the God of Western religion has died. But that word "God" has now been dragged down to the very lowest depths, used to sanction greed, economic inequity, imperialism, war, and the slaughter of innocents to such a great degree that nearly the whole civilized world is ashamed of and disgusted with America, as you can read by scanning stories in the world press.

I can see three logical paths from here, though I think only two are viable and only one can work in the long run. The path that won't work is to abandon religion and everything it stands for and go to war over merely political ideologies, which is a bit of what this last election looked like to me. But at its best, religion is about preserving and claiming ultimacy for the highest ideals we can articulate. And abandoning *that* search seems insane to me.

The second path is the one that the Anglican priest, Reverend Giles Fraser, wants—to try and force normative Christianity back into a path that follows the demanding and revolutionary teachings of Jesus rather than the supernatural myths created around the baby and the cross. This is the path that virtually all Christian scholars and moderate-to-liberal preachers wish they could take—men like Bishop John Shelby Spong and Jim Wallis of the liberal evangelical magazine, *Sojourners*. I wish them luck, but I don't think they can do it this time. It has simply become too painfully clear that, as that Anglican priest said, the religion of Christianity has become far easier to misuse than to use wisely and well.

But this is true of all three Western religions. I think the God of all three Western religions—Judaism, Christianity, and Islam— has become the hand puppet of the worst kind of people and has found its most likely home among them.

Israel acts in violent and murderous ways against Palestinians, ways that the great prophets of the Bible would condemn in a heartbeat. Their God is used for little but a land grant and a sanction for revenge and violence. Meanwhile, the fundamentalists of Islam have dragged the ninety-nine names of Allah through more mud than anyone knows how to remove. They champion a primitive and vicious patriarchy that cannot be defended as being worthy of Allah. They brag about murder and suicide bombers and speak in terms of blood, violence, and death. Muhammad would be disgusted with them. Yet it is difficult to find many voices of moderate or liberal Muslims to counter them. Once again, the God of the Bible has been turned into a barbaric and murderous hand puppet by our worst people, and no one within any of the three religions seems able or willing to stop them.

That's where this reminds me of that music review that Debussy wrote about the Wagner opera. These brutal, ungodly versions of Western religion are clearly holding the reins of power with violence and murder. They are all kings of their respective hills, and their arrogant spokesmen brag that this is the dawning of a new and bloody age, to be played by their rules.

I don't think so. I think these mean, selfish, and arrogant perversions of religion show instead that that symbol, that god, no longer has the power to attract enough decent and brave people to rescue it from the gutters.

Earlier, I mentioned that this happened after Franco finally died and his dictatorship of Spain ended. He had brought the Catholic Church into power with him, and after he died, people began removing power from the church as well. It had proven too easy and eager an ally of low and mean motives to be trusted.

And I think that is what may happen to Christianity in America. I don't know enough about the state of religious affairs in Israel or the Muslim world to talk about them. But I've seen enough bad preachers and politicians here enlist Jesus and God in their greedy, imperialistic, and murderous schemes to believe that the symbol of God may well lose its right to be trusted.

So the third path, the one I think is most interesting, is the chance to reclaim our highest ideals from *institutional* religion and begin expressing them in ordinary language that can belong to all the people. This would reverse the authority of churches and believers, which is exactly what Jesus and the ancient Hebrew prophets also did. It would mean that we would judge the churches by how well they served our ideals, rather than pretending that they have the moral right to judge us in the name of a God they have turned into a greedy mercenary.

This sounds like such a big task, it seems unrealistic to pretend it can be done. But it can be done. In fact, it is being done all the time.

As some of the best theologians have said for centuries, the gods are symbols that we wrap in rituals and creeds, embed in worship services, and trust to guard the better angels of our nature. But the ideals belong to us, not the gods.

About 164 years ago, a great German theologian named Ludwig Feuerbach wrote that all the attributes of the gods are the things that *we* happen to admire, and we project them onto the gods we have created in the same way that we project noble ideals onto our race or our country. And 206 years ago, another theologian, Friedrich Schleiermacher, who was Feuerbach's teacher, wrote that religion is a purely human invention, designed to help us become most fully human. It was, he added, the *most important* of human inventions, when it worked.

This means we have serious work to do.

It means that we as a society need to do what we as individuals do when we leave an inadequate religion. We need to look for more adequate ways to express our ideals in ordinary language, rather than the jargon claimed as the private reserve of churches and preachers. That is the most important religious task I think America now faces: reclaiming our high ideals from religions that have proven unworthy to handle them and too cowardly to speak up for them in any effective way.

Perhaps you think this is beyond you, that you don't know these things, that it's presumptuous to think you might know what's moral and right better than churches with 2,000 years of tradition behind them. It's not true.

All of our hearts opened for people we didn't even know as soon as we heard the tragic story of the tsunami in Southeast Asia start to unfold a few days ago. You don't have to be told they are your brothers and sisters or children of God; you know it intuitively and deeply. It's in your genes. The tender mercies that well up in us toward the suffering of all those people we don't know—they are *our* tender mercies. Not God's, not Jesus's, not Allah's, but *ours*.

Claiming those noble callings is laying claim to our fullest humanity. And all the gods, all the saviors, all the angels we create are not holy in their own right. Their holiness is only on loan from us, as long as they embody our highest aspirations. *We* make the noises, not the gods.

I want us to grow beyond thinking that religion is about bowing before an external source of authority or goodness.

I want us to grow beyond thinking it is the job of priests to proclaim and believers to obey.

I want us to grow into the realization that if there is ever to be an incarnation of truth, justice, and compassion—an incarnation of God—that incarnation must take *our* shape, not the shape of gods, prophets, and saviors who have been dead for a long time.

Some first-rate religious thinkers have said that this is the deepest significance of the Christian myth of Jesus as an incarnation of God. They see early Christianity—unlike the religions that preceded it—as saying that the form that God's presence must take to be effective among us can only be human form, *our* form. No, that's not how literalist religions have taught it. They have taught it as a supernaturalism, which lets them use these powerful symbols to subdue the masses rather than to empower them.

The soul of honest religion is the human soul seeking its own finest form. The soul of all legitimate religion is the human spirit.

I first read this in the Bible. It isn't an obscure piece; it's the ending of the Ninetieth Psalm, one of the best known of all the Psalms. After praising God for a few verses, the psalm ends with a plea. It may strike you almost as antireligious, but it is not. It is the most profoundly religious plea we can make. It is this: "and establish the work of *our* hands upon us; yea, the work of *our* hands; establish thou it" (90:17).

That doesn't mean *any* work of our hands. It doesn't mean the *dirty* work of our hands. It means the work of the hands of those angels of our better nature, the vehicles of our highest and most sacred yearnings. We address those angels, those highest of ideals, and we ask them for the courage of our deepest convictions, saying, "and establish the work of *our* hands upon us; yea, the work of *our* hands, establish thou it."

It's a good place to start, now and always.

POSTLUDE

One of the best metaphors for our situation is the ancient Hindu and Buddhist parable of the blind men and the elephant. Each religion—even at its best—is no more than one of the "blind men," illuminating one part of a larger truth. None of us will ever see life in its totality or see it clearly—we can only "see through a glass, darkly," to use Saint Paul's wonderful phrase. That means there must be as many of us as possible at the table, from all religions (and from relevant secular disciplines), and we must learn to speak to each other in languages that include the tender mercies of the others. Only ordinary language can do this.

The other metaphor that can enlighten us is also Buddhist: that all teachings, teachers, religions, and wise traditions are like fingers pointing at the moon. Our mistake is to worship the finger, the gods of any religion. Our challenge is to see the noble ideals at which the fingers are pointing, and work together to embody them.

Jesus described the kingdom of God as the state of affairs when we all treat one another like brothers, sisters, and children of God. The Buddha taught that our suffering lies mostly in the misleading ways we think of things, and if we free ourselves from the need for our illusions—including our comforting illusions—we might find peace in the world as it really is, and in ourselves as we really are. Islam teaches that Allah sent 124,000 prophets (signifying an infinite number) from Adam to Muhammad, meaning that different religions are bringing the same unique message. That's the kind of mature teaching that makes a tradition great. Most Muslims—though not the violent fanatics masquerading as *jihadis*—would dearly love to see a return to their religion's more humane teachings.

It is imperative that we see—and reclaim—the values and ideals that all our religions aspire to and that we use them to critique our politics, religion, and media. This is not a plea for a "secular" society. It is a plea for a society based on deep and demanding morality and ethics that are being betrayed by our politicians, our preachers, and our pundits.

Voltaire once said, "Those with the power to make you believe absurdities have the power to make you commit atrocities." The danger in literalistic religions is not that they teach people to believe absurdities, but that they prepare them to commit atrocities. Blow people away in the name of the Lord? Kill innocent people in tall buildings and have seventy virgins clamoring to please you? Such statements are both absurd and atrocious.

And so we stand early in this new millennium, a nation goosestepping to fascist drummers beating out the rhythm of the rich, with our political system and our religions hijacked by the worst among us. Meanwhile, the rich get richer and their command-and-control empire destroys much of our hope, our sense of safety, and our belief that our children will have it better than we did.

But fascism can be stopped by people armed with the courage of their convictions—think of that image of the lone Chinese student standing in front of the tank in Tiananmen Square. We are not really alone. The majority of people in our country and around the world can make good allies in an honest and noble cause.

And given the political reality of a GOP-dominated America today, Republicans can be significant allies—they can speak the loudest and have the most influence. While the business and religious leaders of the Republican Party have control of the political system, the vast majority of Republicans are suffering under their own party's policies, watching their life savings vanish, their jobs go overseas, their health care subjected to profit-making, and their security diminished. If the majority of Republicans ever awaken, they may be this administration's most formidable enemy.

All religious Americans, but especially Christians, can also be powerful agents of change—if they take their religion back. Anyone who has read the Bible with a good heart knows it is not the book of bigotry and hatred that the Falwells of the world make it out to be. Christians need to challenge their churches and insist that they preach and practice the radical kind of love that Jesus represented, not the low and mean religion of our worst ministers.

Besides the religious and the Republican, other allies must come from the new silent majority of the 60 to 80 percent of Americans who have not gone to church regularly in decades. They need to take the prophetic role of reclaiming high ideals from the priests. Paradoxically, this group can play the most "religious" role of all—like the prophets in the Hebrew scriptures who came from the countryside to denounce the religion of the priests as immoral and unfaithful. It isn't clear that the major prophets attended or cared much for the formal religious services of their day. Yet the highest moral standards of Western religions were spoken by the prophets, not the priests. The same can be true today.

As for the Democrats and those on the political left—they can affect change if they can grow past the individual rights language of the 1960s and find a way to reclaim the most important vocabularies in America: nationalism, patriotism, religion, morality, and personal responsibility.

Writing an "ending" to this little book seems premature. We don't need an ending; we need a beginning. The majority of good people in America have been lulled into inaction, even put to sleep, and we have slept for far too long. As we slept, the world around us was redefined from a nominal democracy into a proto-fascist state that is slowly moving closer to a full-fledged fascist America each day. Can we—will we—wake up and act before it is simply too late? I honestly don't know—it often seems unlikely. But I hope and pray that we can and will, for everything, absolutely everything, depends on it.